THE LITTLE BOOK OF
CONCORDE

Written by **David Curnock**

THE LITTLE BOOK OF
CONCORDE

This edition first published in the UK in 2007
by Green Umbrella Publishing

© Green Umbrella Publishing 2009

www.gupublishing.co.uk

Publishers Jules Gammond, Vanessa Gardner

Printed and bound in Poland

ISBN 978-1-905828-86-9

Contents

Chapter 1

Entente Concordable

Entente \ en'tente, n. [French, from Old French, intent, from feminine past participle of entendre, to understand, intend.] An agreement between two or more governments or powers for co-operative action or policy.

Concordable \ Con'cord'a'ble\, a. [L. concordabilis.] Capable of according; agreeing; harmonious. Translates into French with the same spelling and meaning.

SHORTLY AFTER 1PM GMT ON November 26 2003, Concorde G-BOAF touched down at her birthplace in Filton, Bristol. As this iconic airliner settled gently onto the runway for her final landing, the duty air traffic controller brought an historic era to a close with the words, "Welcome home, Concorde". Thus ended a chapter in aviation history that had begun more than half a century earlier.

The British Studies

BRITISH GOVERNMENT INTEREST in supersonic flight can be traced back to 1943 with the issue of a specification for a 'transonic' aircraft capable of Mach 1.5 (approximately 1,000 miles per hour) at an altitude of 36,500 feet. However, the ensuing Miles M.52 design was controversially cancelled, as it neared completion, early in 1946 and a programme using air-launched models took its place. In cancelling the

M.52, the Air Ministry Director of Scientific Research, Sir Ben Lockspeiser, said: "...in view of the unknown hazards near the speed of sound ... [it is] considered unwise to proceed with the full-scale experiments." The design material and data from the M.52 project was made available to the American Bell Aircraft company. In parallel research, in America, the quest for higher speeds continued, leading to the first 'intentional' supersonic flight by Captain Chuck Yeager in the rocket-powered Bell X-1 in 1947.

ABOVE Last landing for Concorde G-BOAF at Filton, November 26 2003

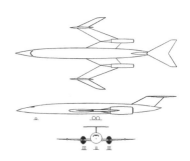

Post-war Britain had lost its lead in world aviation and strove to regain its prestige with some bold decisions involving government ministries, the aviation industry, and airlines. At Farnborough, the Royal Aircraft Establishment (RAE) had carried out much research into supersonic flight and was in the forefront of proposals to establish a committee to direct Britain's efforts in the development of a supersonic airliner. Its deputy director, (later, Sir) Morien Morgan, became chairman of the Supersonic Transport Aircraft Committee (STAC) when it was set up in 1956.

Early in 1959, the STAC was able to recommend the development of two types of supersonic airliner. One was for a 100-seat aircraft with a cruising speed of Mach 1.2 (800 miles per hour) and a range of 1,500 miles. The other was for a 150-seater with a cruising speed of Mach 1.8 (1,200 miles per hour) and a range of 3,500 miles for transatlantic routes. The government placed the medium-range project on hold but awarded development contracts to various companies to study possible configurations for the long-range proposal.

Early research work and wind tunnel results showed that the configuration with the most promise was that with a plan form of a slender delta wing. This layout offered the most advantages of all the shapes explored. There was an additional benefit in that the slender delta offered an increase in aerodynamic efficiency at speeds of up to Mach 2.2. Feasibility studies carried out jointly by Hawker-Siddeley Aviation and British Aircraft Corporation (BAC) into the delta wing concept came up with two radically different designs. The Hawker proposal was for an aircraft with a thick delta wing with an integral fuselage, while the BAC version featured a thin wing with a conventionally mounted slender fuselage. Comparison of the two designs found in favour of the BAC proposal and a design study contract was awarded.

The BAC offering was the Bristol Type 198 that had previously been submitted by the Bristol Aeroplane Company for the initial feasibility study prior to that company being absorbed into the BAC organisation in 1960. The Type 198 was of slender delta plan form, and was to have been powered by six Olympus turbojet engines. With transatlantic range, it was designed to carry 130 passengers and had a maximum weight of 380.000 pounds at take-off.

difficulties and the economic disadvantages of having six engines, led to its rejection. The government instead called for a smaller, 100-seat aircraft, which resulted in the proposal for the Bristol Type 223. This aircraft would have a maximum take-off weight of 250,000 pounds, be powered by four Olympus engines, and would carry 100 passengers over transatlantic range.

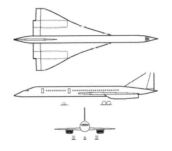

MIDDLE Drawing of the Bristol Type 198 proposal for a supersonic airliner

LEFT General arrangement of the Bristol Type 223

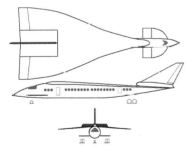

A combination of factors, largely concerning its greater weight, which increased the 'sonic boom' effect, coupled with engine intake design

The government design study also called for the active consideration by BAC of the possibility for an international partnership to collaborate on the project. There were obvious benefits in such collaboration with particular regard to the requirement for manpower resources, research and development facilities, and production capacity. The financial burden would also be too heavy for a single government to underwrite on its own. Therefore, BAC invited participation by France, Germany and the United States. The latter two countries declined; Germany considered the challenge too great for its aircraft industry at that time, whereas the USA was more interested in furthering its own Mach 3 project that was based on the XB-70 Valkyrie bomber. However, France was not dismissive of the partnership idea.

The French Connection

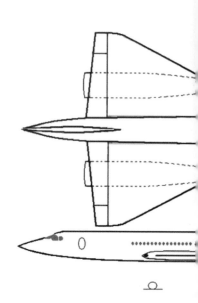

RUNNING IN PARALLEL WITH THE work in Britain, the French had also been investigating the feasibility of supersonic air transport. In the forefront of their work in this field was the French manufacturer, Sud-Aviation. In 1957, together with Dassault and Nord-Aviation, and with input from Air France, the three companies began to study the possibilities of supersonic air transport. Like its counterpart in Britain, the former Bristol Aeroplane Company, Sud-Aviation had also been subjected to merger when it became part of the SNIAS group, with the name that was soon to become known throughout the world, Aerospatiale.

The French consortium had concentrated their efforts on a medium-range supersonic aircraft, known as the

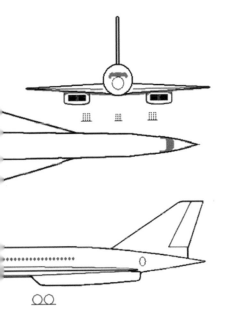

LEFT The proposed Sud-Aviation Super-Caravelle was remarkably similar in configuration to that of the Bristol Type 223

longer-range model. The French project differed mainly in the respect of range from that of the British proposal, with BAC being firmly of the opinion that the journey time benefits of supersonic flight would best be found over sectors of transatlantic length. When BAC raised its government-imposed requirement for a programme partner, the French company was receptive to the possibility of collaboration but only on the basis that there would be two types of aircraft, one medium-range, and one long-range.

During 1961, BAC and Sud-Aviation submitted their respective proposals for a long-range and a medium-range aircraft. Although the objectives were broadly similar, there were key differences in some areas of design. However, by this time, consultations between the two governments had already taken place and their findings concluded that there was insufficient 'joint working' in either company's proposal.

Super-Caravelle. Drawing upon their experience with the successful Caravelle medium-range airliner, Sud Aviation was of the opinion that a long-range aircraft would be a step too far and believed that a medium-range version was a more achievable objective. If this project was to prove successful, their experience could then be applied to a

Agreement is Reached

FOLLOWING A FORMAL MEETING between the French and British at the June 1961 Paris Air Show, and subsequent ministerial-level negotiations, both countries signed an historic agreement on November 29 1962. The following extract is taken from the first part of the document:

"The Government of the United Kingdom of Great Britain and Northern Ireland and the Government of the French Republic.

Having decided to develop and produce jointly a civil supersonic transport aircraft; have agreed as follows:

Article 1

(1) The principle of this collaboration shall be equal sharing between the two countries, on the basis of equal responsibility for the project as a whole, of the work, of the expenditure income by the two Governments, and of the proceeds of sales. (This clause effectively made the project 'uncancelable' by either government).

(2) This principle, which shall be observed as strictly as possible – shall apply, as regards both development and production (including spares), to the project considered as a whole (airframe, engine, system and equipment)."

Further, it stated that the development of both the medium-range and long-range versions was to be given equal priority. It formalised the establishment of integrated organisations to carry out the airframe and the engine aspects of the work, and the setting up of a Standing Committee with members from both participating countries to oversee the project. The document went on to ratify the separate agreements made between Sud-Aviation and British Aircraft Corporation on October 25 1962, and between Bristol Siddeley Engines and Société Nationale d'Etude et de Construction de Moteurs d'Aviation (SNECMA) on November 28 1961, for collaboration on the airframe and engine projects, respectively.

Project funding was to be underwritten, and shared equally, between the two governments. Although it had previously been agreed that the project was to embrace both the medium-range and long-range versions of the aircraft,

discussions with potential airline customers cast doubts on the viability of the medium-range aircraft, which was then cancelled.

Early in 1965 the preliminary design was frozen and the construction of two prototypes, one in each country, commenced.

Chapter 2

Research and Test Aircraft

PRIOR TO THE FORMATION OF the British Aircraft Corporation (BAC) its predecessor aircraft manufacturing companies had already carried out much of the early design work for a British supersonic airliner. Some of this work eventually found its way into the joint Anglo-French project that was to become Concorde. French aircraft manufacturing companies had also ventured into projects that gave them the confidence to propose their own supersonic airliner project. It was no coincidence that the efforts of the British and French designers came up with similar configurations for their supersonic airliner proposals. These designs were based around the 'delta wing' configuration.

The Delta Wing

THE DELTA WING IS NOT A modern invention, predating the first successful manned, powered flight by almost 40 years. In 1867, the first British patent for such a design was granted to two Englishmen, J W Butler and E Edwards, for their proposed steam-powered flying machine. In the same year a Russian engineer, Nicolai de Teleschoff, took out a French patent for an aeroplane 'representing' an equilateral triangle. Others were also inspired to experiment with the delta wing, notably in Germany in the late 1920s, on hang-gliders

and various tail-less sailplanes.

In 1931, the Frenchman Nicolas-Roland Payen was granted a French patent for his 'autoplan' PA 100 aircraft whose principal flying surface was a wing in the shape of an isosceles triangle. This aircraft was named Delta, as it resembled the form of the fourth letter

ABOVE Avro 698 Vulcan, a revolutionary four-jet Delta bomber, 1952

RIGHT Three-view drawing of the Payen PA100, 1931

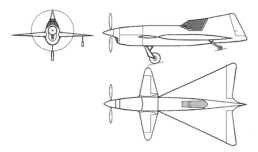

in the Greek alphabet, and featured canard fore-planes. Following several high-profile crashes in Germany, including the tragic death of the sailplane pilot Gunter Groenhoff while piloting a Delta IX at Rhon in 1932, the German Luftwaffe Ministerium (Air Ministry) prohibited the construction of this kind of apparatus "… as it was not suitable for development and had no practical value."

Ironically, one of those in the forefront of the delta wing researchers was Professor Alexander Lippisch, a German, who had investigated the aerodynamics of the delta during the 1930s. During World War 2, the delta concept was resurrected, and tested extensively in wind tunnels. This work by Lippisch led to the development of the Messerschmitt Me 163 Komet rocket-propelled fighter in the early 1940s. This aircraft was of tail-less delta planform, with no horizontal stabilisers, a feature common with most delta wing designs. Lippisch later went to the United States where he worked on military supersonic flight projects.

The principal advantage of a delta wing is its ability to provide high lift in supersonic flight. However, there are significant disadvantages, including the requirement for much higher take-off and landing speeds, its relative instability at high angles of attack, and poor low-speed performance. Each of these aspects needed to be fully explored, and the resultant data incorporated into the design of any proposed supersonic airliner, together with the in-flight testing of any engine that was intended to power such an aircraft.

The French were convinced that the delta wing afforded the best means of achieving supersonic performance. They produced a series of experimental aircraft, including the Sud-Est SE212 Durandal that flew supersonically in

1957. This aircraft achieved a speed of Mach 1.37, powered by its jet engine, and Mach 1.57 with the assistance of a rocket motor. Further developments within France eventually led to the production of one of the world's most successful fighter aircraft, the delta-winged Dassault Mirage. Their years of experience in this field stood the French aircraft industry in good stead when applied to the supersonic airliner project.

The Avro 707 Series

IN 1947, DURING DESIGN STUDIES for the Avro 698 jet-engine bomber that was to become the Vulcan, it was determined that the best solution would be that of a delta-shaped wing with no horizontal tail-plane. Although there would be advantages in performance, this configuration had not previously been flown on any British aircraft. In order to explore the handling of this type of aircraft, the Avro 707 series of research aircraft was developed, and the

first aircraft flew in September 1949.

A 1/3rd-scale model of the proposed Type 698, the Avro 707 programme was blighted with problems and was too late to provide a major contribution to the Vulcan programme. It did, however, provide much valuable data on the general handling and flight characteristics of the delta wing. The Vulcan itself was later to make its own valuable contribution to the supersonic airliner project. Of the five aircraft built, two examples of the Avro 707 exist in the UK, one in the Manchester Museum of Science and Industry and one in the RAF Museum, Cosford. A third example is preserved in Australia at the RAAF Museum, Point Cook.

BELOW Layout of the Sud-Est SE212 Durandal

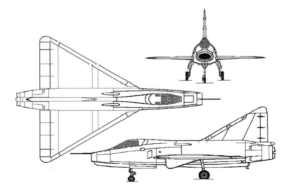

Boulton Paul P.111

THE BOULTON PAUL P.111 MADE its first flight in October 1950. This aircraft was designed to investigate the behaviour of the delta wing at transonic speeds. Fitted with detachable tips to its wings and vertical fin, a number of different wing and fin shapes were tested across the transonic speed range. The wing tips gave it a span varying between 25ft 8in and 33ft 6in according to the shape under test. Being particularly sensitive in handling, and alluding to its high-visibility paint scheme, this aircraft was known to its test pilots as the 'Yellow Peril'. Modified to become the P.111a, after a wheels-up landing, this aircraft is exhibited in the collection of the Midlands Aircraft Preservation Society at Baginton, Coventry.

Handley Page HP115

FLOWN FOR THE FIRST TIME IN August 1961, the HP115 was designed to explore the low-speed characteristics of a slender delta wing form. It featured a 74° swept-wing with provision for other angles of sweep to be tested. With a top speed of around 300 miles per hour, this aircraft had a length of 45 feet, and a very low-aspect wing with a span of only 20 feet. This unique aircraft is on display alongside Concorde 002 at the Fleet Air Arm Museum, RNAS Yeovilton.

RIGHT Handley Page HP115 low-speed delta-wing research aircraft

BAC 221

THE BAC 221 AIRCRAFT STARTED life as the Fairey Delta 2 (FD2), one of two built in response to a Ministry of Supply specification for a transonic and supersonic aircraft. Originally fitted with a standard delta wing this aircraft, WG 774, was first flown in October 1954 by Peter Twiss and later became the first to exceed 1,000 miles per hour. In March 1956, with the same pilot, it broke the World Absolute Speed record at 1,132 miles per hour, near Littlehampton, in Sussex.

Because of the high angle of attack required to provide sufficient lift at the slower end of its speed range, ie for take-off and landing, the delta wing configuration dictated that the nose undercarriage was of necessity longer than usual to provide the optimum angle of attack in those phases of flight.

For high-speed flight, the aerodynamics dictated a long slender nose. This obstructed forward vision so, in order to improve visibility during the take-off and landing phases of flight, the nose and cockpit assembly was arranged such that it could be drooped by 10°. A similar arrangement for its nose, but not its cockpit, was to become a feature of the Concorde design.

In 1960, WG774 was converted by BAC from its original 'triangular' delta wing form to that of a slender ogee delta, with the object of simulating the wing planform of the proposed British supersonic airliner project. This aircraft was used in research into the effects of transonic and supersonic flight, and made many flights between 1964 and 1973. It is currently exhibited at the Fleet Air Arm Museum, RNAS Yeovilton.

BELOW Test nacelle on Vulcan XA903 showing the Olympus 593 engine installation. The moveable intake ramp is the white panel at the top of the intake duct and the auxiliary intake door at the bottom is in the open position

Avro Vulcan XA903

IN MAY 1957, THE FIFTEENTH Vulcan B Mk1 to leave the production line, XA903, took off on its maiden flight from Woodford, near Manchester. This particular aircraft was destined never to fly in RAF squadron service as it had already been earmarked as the test aircraft that would be modified to carry the Avro Blue Steel standoff nuclear weapon. Included in the modifications for its role with Blue Steel were new avionics equipment and a Vulcan B Mk2 nose undercarriage leg. After being fitted with new partially recessed bomb bay doors and other equipment

at Langar, XA903 returned to Woodford in January 1958 for the Blue Steel test programme.

After completion of her duties with the Blue Steel project, this aircraft was assigned to Bristol Siddeley's Flight Test Division at Filton, where it arrived on January 3 1964. XA903 was to replace its predecessor XA894 that had been destroyed in a fire while ground running. The modified bomb bay, coupled with the Vulcan's high ground clearance, formed an ideal basis for the siting of the Olympus 593 engine that was to be installed for flight-testing. The 593 engine was a much-improved development of the Olympus 200 and 300 series of engines that were used to power the test-bed Vulcan itself, as well as those in squadron service with the Royal Air Force.

The test installation for the Olympus 593 was effectively one-half of a Concorde nacelle and was mounted underneath the bomb bay. Fuel and water tanks, together with engine test instrumentation and control equipment were fitted within the bomb bay. The right hand side of the nacelle carried a representation of the Concorde nacelle central splitter plate that projected forward of the intake. Fitted with a moveable intake ramp and auxiliary intake door, the test nacelle could, for test purposes, represent both a Number 1, or Number 2, engine installation on Concorde. After two years of conversion work, and several weeks of ground running, XA903 flew again on September 9 1966 and made an appearance on the last two days of the Farnborough Air Show. However, the Olympus 593 test engine was not run in the air until after the show.

Although the Vulcan could be flown using only the power of the Olympus 593 itself, in practice the aircraft's main engines were never shut down, as they were needed to supply the vital electrical power for the aircraft systems. The modifications and test equipment had substantially increased the maximum landing weight above that of a standard Vulcan B Mk1. The low-mounted ventral test nacelle precluded the use of aerodynamic braking in which the aircraft nose is held high during the landing roll to reduce speed. Therefore, the Vulcan brake parachute was streamed on every one of the 219 landings during the test programme. However, on landing after its final Olympus 593 test flight, the braking parachute failed to deploy properly, and then failed to jettison when the landing was aborted, and a go-around was initiated. The parachute continued to trail behind the aircraft for several circuits of the airfield before falling away in shreds, after which a successful landing was made.

A total of 417 flying hours were flown during the Olympus 593 programme including 248 engine test hours. After the final Olympus 593 test flight on July 21 1971, XA903 was sent to Marshall's of Cambridge for its test nacelle to be converted to receive the Rolls-Royce RB199 engine that was destined for the Panavia Multi-Role Combat (MRCA) aircraft, later named the Panavia Tornado. Sadly, only the nose section of this historic Vulcan aircraft has been preserved. This is now in private ownership and can be viewed at the Wellesbourne Wartime Museum, near Stratford-upon-Avon.

ABOVE Vulcan XA903 flight-testing the Bristol Siddeley-Snecma Olympus 593 engine. Note the truncated rear fuselage housing the brake parachute

Chapter 3

Turning Theory into Practice

AFTER THE NECESSARY AGREE-ments had been signed between the respective governments, and under the watchful eyes of the Standing Committee, the realisation of the project was left to the combined efforts of the main contractors. These were the two airframe manufacturers, Sud-Aviation (later, Aerospatiale) of France and the British Aircraft Corporation (BAC), together with the two engine companies, Bristol Siddeley (later, Rolls Royce) and SNECMA of France. This mammoth task was almost overpowering in its concept, not only in the realm of technical design but also in the planning for manufacture of component parts, and their subsequent assembly into a complete airliner. With over 100,000 detail parts drawings alone, this meant that a great deal of collaboration was required between the various partners, especially with regard to the interfaces between their respective prime assemblies. There was also much input from the various component and system manufacturers without whom the project would not have succeeded. Although there were some inevitable problems to be reconciled, either due to language or differing work practices, the partnership

between the main contractors eventually succeeded in forging a bond that has lasted into the present century. This working relationship has carried through, from Concorde, to the Airbus series of aircraft and other collaborative projects.

LEFT Early mock-up of nose and visor, Filton 1965

Sharing the Workload

THE INITIAL DEVELOPMENT costs had been estimated at between £150–£170 million. Responsibility for the airframe was in the proportion of 40:60 British and French, with those proportions reversed for the engine work. The lion's share of airframe work was biased in favour of the French because the British already held the majority-share in the engine programme.

Production and final assembly were concentrated at two main airframe manufacturing sites both, coincidentally, being located in the south-western region of the respective partner countries, Toulouse in France, and

RIGHT Over-optimistic
first flight target date.
Concorde 001's maiden
flight took place on
March 2 1969

Filton, near Bristol. Each manufacturer was responsible for a particular part of the aircraft, there being no duplication of airframe production jigs, although both sites had their own final production line. Completed sections of the aircraft were then transported between sites for final assembly, a considerable task in itself. This international method of construction is commonly used today, particularly in the manufacture of the Airbus series of aircraft.

Main areas of responsibility for Sud-Aviation included the design, development and production of the fuselage rear cabin and main wing sections, wing control surfaces and associated flying controls, hydraulic systems, air conditioning system, radio and navigation systems. The outer wing sections and some of the control surfaces were sub-contracted to Dassault, while Hispano-Suiza and Messier were tasked with the production of the undercarriage assemblies. The automatic flight control system was sub-contracted out jointly to Marconi (later, GEC-Marconi) of Britain and the French company SFENA (later, Sextant Avionique).

BAC was responsible for the three forward fuselage sections, the rear fuselage and vertical tail surfaces, engine nacelles and inlet ducts, engine/airframe integration, the fuel, oxygen, fire warning and extinguishing systems, and the sound and thermal insulation. The forward fuselage and nose section, which was around 50 feet in length, and

EVRIER 1968
SA REALISATION

Prototype **001**

and nozzle sections being provided by SNECMA. Much development work had already been done by Bristol Siddeley to improve both the power and reliability of the Olympus engine so it was, therefore, logical that they should continue to lead that part of the programme. The Olympus was no stranger to the high-altitude environment that was to be the realm of Concorde, having powered a Canberra bomber when it set a world altitude record of 65,889 feet in 1955.

Costs, Communication and Transport

ONE OF THE FIRST DIFFICULTIES to be overcome was that of language, both English and French. The British are renowned the world over for their reticence in embracing a foreign language even though French, in particular, had been on the school curriculum in Britain for many years. Conversation is one thing, but technical

the rear fuselage and fin unit were produced at the BAC Weybridge factory, in Surrey.

Engine development and production was shared between Bristol Siddeley, for the Olympus 593 engine itself, with the reheat (afterburner) system, exhaust

BELOW Concorde
prototype 001 during
build at Toulouse,
January 1967

language is another, more difficult, aspect of any foreign tongue. The French, with their experience in demonstrating and marketing the Caravelle and other aircraft around the world, had a

head start as many of their negotiations had been undertaken in what had become the international language of the aviation world, English. Although there were problems at first, mainly due

to misplaced national pride, the project progressed albeit somewhat hesitantly on the verbal communications front. Differences were soon overcome and it became commonplace for meetings to be held bi-lingually, with engineers from both countries speaking in their own language without real-time translation. Another major difference between the two nations was in staff etiquette and relationships, where the informal use of first names, by the British, was at odds with the more formal manner of address used by the French.

In today's high-tech environment it is difficult to imagine how the working practices of the Concorde programme were communicated between the respective partners and their sub contractors. The facility of the email and internet of today was almost unimaginable to the groundbreaking pioneers of the supersonic airliner. Even the telephone systems of the day were comparatively crude, with the exception of the satellite telephone. Much of the correspondence was carried out using ordinary mail services that were slow and unreliable, so a shuttle air service was instigated between the two main centres. Engineers and their support staffs often made the journey between the two countries for meetings and 'hands-on' experience of the hardware. This practice has been carried through from the Concorde project to the workings of the partners in the Airbus consortium in the present day.

The requirement to shuttle engineering staff between the two centres, on a daily basis, as well as the need to transport completed sub-assemblies to their respective assembly lines all added significantly to the programme costs, the original estimates being somewhat over-optimistic. Additional costs were incurred due to inflation, and the high interest rates that prevailed during the 1970s. The world oil price leapt dramatically four-fold in 1973, causing many to doubt the commercial viability of Concorde. Coupled with a general rise in interest rates that reached 24% in the UK, against around 5% in France during 1975, the value of the pound falling by almost one-third in five years, and general unrest in the labour market, it was almost miraculous that the project survived at all.

From the original £150–170 million estimated, the total cost for development of Concorde was around £1.134 billion, this sum being borne in equal amounts by the governments, and taxpayers, of Britain and France. Added to that sum, the production costs for the 16 airline versions of the aircraft were a further £654 million, offset by the sum of around £278 million that was received from the customers in sales revenues.

New Techniques and Work Practices

ONCE THE REALISATION HAD SET in that neither country could have achieved the goal on its own, the desire for the programme to succeed overcame national differences in a number of areas. Not least of these was the matter of the two different standards of measurement used by the partner countries, imperial and metric. Each country used its own system of measurement when drawing the parts of the design for which it was responsible. French originated parts were designed in metric units; those from Britain were drawn using imperial measurements. Structural interfaces between the parts were dimensioned in both standards, a simple but time-consuming compromise. Together with a unified drawing office numbering system, the design process was underway,

and the programme moved forward to the manufacture of detail parts and assemblies.

In a major departure from previous aircraft production methods many new engineering and construction techniques were brought into use.

Whereas previous airframe fabrication methods relied to a large extent on either riveted skins and strengthening ribs and stringers, or welding, the technique known as 'sculpture' or integral milling was adopted for many of the structural parts used in Concorde. This method involved the milling of material, from solid billets of metal, using CNC (Computer Numerically Controlled) tape-controlled milling machines. The process was found to be extremely accurate, and offered great strength-to-weight ratio advantages over conventional methods as weight saving was one of the main engineering considerations throughout the project. There was a further benefit in that the use of this method could also potentially reduce labour costs, although this was partly negated by the need to transport assemblies between the two countries.

Apart from the high-grade aluminium alloy Hiduminium RR 58 that was used in the main structures, titanium and stainless steel were also used in areas that were highly stressed or subjected to great heat, especially around the engine bays. In order to use these materials in Concorde, new processes needed to be

LEFT Wooden mock-ups under construction at Filton

RIGHT An early
mock-up of the
front end

developed or existing methods refined. With particular reference to titanium, this material was notoriously difficult to weld, as it required pinpoint accuracy in order to prevent weakening or distortion to the surrounding material. To this end, the development of electron beam welding was perfected to such a degree as to enable components to be built up with welding, thus allowing smaller, lighter and more cost efficient items to be manufactured than hitherto. Advanced laser-controlled tooling was developed along with chemical etching and explosion forming of materials. These innovations led the way for the production techniques used both in aircraft manufacture and elsewhere, in the late 20th and early 21st centuries.

Another innovation, due largely to the political requirement for a dual production-line system, was the delivery of fully equipped sub-assemblies for final assembly. This involved the installation of most electrical wiring, flying controls, hydraulics, air-conditioning and insulation components as the sections of aircraft were being built, thus requiring comparatively little work on the final

production line other than the necessary connections to be made between the various mating sections.

From Paper Aeroplane to Wooden Model

THE INTERFACES AND RELATIONships between the individual component parts of an assembly can often be better understood by seeing the items 'in the

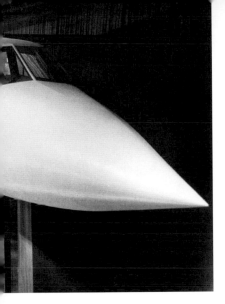

Other models and mock-ups were used for various purposes during the project, including one for the cockpit that was used for instrumentation and equipment layout arrangements. The input from airline pilots and the Concorde test crews was important in the cockpit design where the layout of controls and instrumentation is crucial to the safe operation of the aircraft. The design philosophy of keeping flight deck procedures as near as possible to those used in a conventional aircraft had a major bearing on the flight deck layout. The complimentary comments received from airline pilots during the flight-testing phase proved that the designers' aims had been met.

flesh', rather than on a drawing or sketch. An overall impression of the finished article can also be gained from observation and comparison with a scale replica. In the days before computer-aided design and 3-d graphics, the construction of engineering models and mock-ups was commonplace. The Concorde project was no exception; one of the first items to be produced was a full-scale wooden mock-up. This proved invaluable in the design and manufacturing process, the Filton mock-up being available to engineers as it stood in the assembly hall where Concorde was built.

Mock-ups of cabin layouts were of particular importance to the sales team, enabling them to show prospective customers the interior layout and passenger cabin furnishings. A full size wooden mock-up was exhibited at the Paris Air Show in 1967, giving the public its first glimpse of the airliner of the future. The dream was one step closer to reality, but many challenges were still to be faced in the quest for a supersonic airliner.

Chapter 4

Prototypes and Static Test Airframes

IN THE DEVELOPMENT OF THE world's first supersonic airliner, there were many unknowns to be explored, and design calculations to be verified or validated. Once the materials had been selected, it was necessary to carry out an exhaustive programme of laboratory tests to reproduce the supersonic flight environment, both in terms of the thermal cycles that they would be subjected to, and the structural loading and resistance to fatigue of the articles under test. An understanding of the thermal demands of the supersonic flight profile could be gained from extensive laboratory testing. The rapid rise in the temperature of materials during acceleration, coupled with the prolonged heat-soak in supersonic cruise, followed by rapid cooling under deceleration, could all be reproduced using relatively small articles in the laboratory. Because of the pioneering nature of the project, it was decided to build two test airframes, one for the purposes of static testing, and another for fatigue testing. The use of these test airframes would provide valuable data relating to the ability of the production machines to withstand the rigours of supersonic flight and give confirmation of the calculated in-service life of the complete aircraft.

Static Testing

THE PRINCIPLE OF STATIC TEST-
ing is to ensure that the structural
integrity of the airframe is such that it
can withstand the numerous mechani-
cal, aerodynamic and thermal loads
imposed on it during flight. With the
exception of thermal testing, which was
unique to the Concorde project, static

testing was, and still is, relatively
commonplace in the aeronautics
industry, and is widely accepted as
being valid, and necessary, for all
passenger airliners.

Static testing was undertaken at
Le Centre d'Essais Aéronautiques de
Toulouse (CEAT), Toulouse, and
began in September 1969. Initially, the
airframe was subjected to progressively
increasing load tests at room ambient

ABOVE Static test fuselage and centre wing section roll-out at Toulouse, March 1966

temperature. When the structure had been examined and deemed to have passed these tests, it was then subjected to a series of tests that were repeated alternately between the calculated in-flight temperatures and the ambient, thus replicating the supersonic thermal cycle. Testing was achieved using a vast array of equipment. A series of 80 servo-controlled hydraulic jacks applied the sequenced test loads on the airframe, and a total of 35,000 infra-red lamps provided the necessary means to simulate the effects of heat in the supersonic regime. In order to reduce the skin temperature from over 120°C to -10°C within 15 minutes, thus emulating the flight situation, around 70,000 litres of

Fatigue Testing

AS WELL AS THE STATIC TESTS, there is a requirement to ensure that the structural integrity of the airframe is maintained throughout the life of the aircraft. In isolation, the number of hours flown is no longer a sufficiently adequate indicator of the condition of an aircraft, as the stresses imposed by the number of landings, cabin pressurisation cycles, and in-flight manoeuvres can all be measured, and must be taken into account. Most aircraft are fitted with a 'fatigue meter' that records many of the physical stresses involved in flight operations. The information recorded is compared against data gained from the fatigue testing of a representative airframe in order that an assessment of its absolute fatigue status, and remaining operational life, can be made. Conventional airliners are not usually subjected to extremes of temperature, as in the case of Concorde.

Fatigue testing of the Concorde airframe was, at the time, the most complex and exhaustive ever carried out. At the Royal Aircraft

liquid nitrogen were used. Instrumentation recorded and processed data from 8,000 different points every two seconds.

This initial programme reached its successful conclusion in 1972, when the aircraft was cleared for flight at a take-off weight of 385,000 pounds. Further testing resulted in an increase in the take-off weight to 400,000 pounds.

RIGHT Fatigue
test airframe in rig
at Farnborough, 1973

Establishment, Farnborough, the airframe was surrounded by a jacket that formed a duct around the aircraft through which hot or cold air could be circulated to replicate the thermal cycles of supersonic flight. Five fans, each rated at 2,300 horsepower, pumped the air through the jacket. Warm air was provided by hot water heat exchangers and cold air was supplied via refrigeration units. Around 100 servo-controlled hydraulic jacks were used both to simulate external loading on the airframe and internal loading caused by cabin pressurisation cycles, air-conditioning, and fuel transfer stresses.

Earlier tests had provided evidence that, if the maximum temperature for testing was increased, this would result in a reduction in the time taken to achieve the effects of heat soak and thus reduce the overall test period. Effectively, every hour under test was equivalent to a typical three-hour flight. Progress was fairly rapid; having commenced in August 1973, the certification requirement of 6,800 cycles was achieved by the end of 1975. Subsequent testing was carried out at a yearly rate of 7,000 cycles to maintain the fatigue life of the test specimen at around three times that of the fleet 'fatigue leader' aircraft in airline service.

Miscellaneous Test Facilities

MANY OF THE CONCORDE SYStems and components were tested in specially constructed ground test rigs, including those for the fuel system, electrical system, flying controls, air-conditioning system, and power plant. A full replica of the hydraulic system was built at Toulouse to test operation of the complete aircraft systems including the powered flying control units, undercarriage, and their associated electrical and instrumentation components.

An air intake test facility added to information gained during the Olympus flight test programme, its innovative and automatically controlled variable-ramp system being crucial to supersonic flight as this phase of flight could not be explored in the Vulcan test aircraft. The requirement to reduce the velocity of a large mass of air travelling at speeds of up to Mach 2.2 to around 500 miles per hour, the optimum figure for engine operation, within an intake duct length of around 11 feet was a tremendous challenge to the engineers involved. The Concorde air intake control system is itself a masterpiece in design engineering and ingenuity, and took many hours of testing in rigs and wind tunnels before it could finally be tested in flight, on the prototype aircraft.

Along with individual items that were tested under similar thermal cycles to that of the test airframes, there were the usual bird impact tests on cockpit windows and engines, as well as hailstone impact testing of the whole aircraft structure. The effects of acoustic vibration on the rear fuselage and tail structure were also analysed. At Filton, a sophisticated fuel system test rig was built. This rig was mounted on a platform that could be tilted to simulate changes in the aircraft attitude and the associated effect on the fuel management system, in all flight phases, and at realistic fuel temperatures and pressures. All of these test facilities provided valuable information that enabled any design problems to be corrected before the aircraft flew, thus saving on flight development time.

The enormity of the project is reflected in the amount of time taken to validate the basic aircraft configuration. Using various wind tunnels to cover the subsonic, transonic and supersonic areas of the flight envelope, it took over 5,000 hours of wind tunnel testing and research to validate the basic aerodynamic shape of the aircraft. During this time, the design was refined and enlarged but remained substantially unchanged from the original 'frozen' design.

Simulators

AN AIRCRAFT FLIGHT SIMULATOR not only provides valuable flight crew training facilities but is also an important tool during the design stage of any new aircraft type. This was especially true on the Concorde project where it

RIGHT Modified nose and visor used on post-prototype aircraft

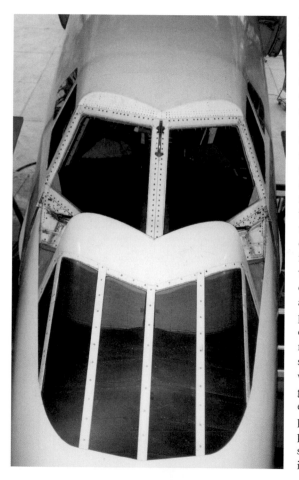

became one of the most advanced simulators in the world at that time. The Filton site was host to a comparatively simple design-aid simulator that was used for the resolution of particular design case studies and testing. The Toulouse simulator was a much more complex item that, in addition to its use to study flight control response and flying characteristics, was also used in the development of new air traffic control procedures. These procedures were needed to manage the Concorde supersonic flights and, when subsonic, integrate them into the existing air traffic patterns. For this purpose, the Toulouse simulator was linked into the air traffic control system at Orly airport, Paris. It was also used for some flight crew training but its principal purpose was as a design aid.

Prototypes and Pre-production Aircraft

DUE TO THE RADICALLY DIFFERent flight regime that Concorde was designed for, there was a need for more than just the two prototype aircraft to carry out testing. From the outset, a further two pre-production aircraft were planned to be built. These additional aircraft would be used to incorporate refinements to the overall aircraft design, and also to develop and evaluate the production methods to be used when building customer's aircraft. The human aspects of Concorde operations from the standpoint of the flight crew were also taken into consideration. Prospective airline customers were consulted, and input from experienced flight crews was taken fully into account.

Concorde was designed from the outset to be flown by a crew of three: pilot, co-pilot and flight engineer. The design was driven by the desire for normal operational practice to be observed, where possible, and this was reflected in the layout of the flight deck that was broadly similar to that of conventional airliners of the era. Most of the controls and instruments showed familiar representation, thus easing the conversion of flight crews onto this otherwise dramatically different aircraft. Crew workload was eased by an array of automated systems, most of which were duplicated. These included two integrated flight-director/auto-pilot systems, two auto-throttle systems, an auto-stabilisation system that eased pilot workload, especially in the event of engine failure and also enhanced the comfort of the passenger in turbulent flight conditions. Duplex air-data systems and an automatic landing capability were also features of the design. As in any new aircraft, all aspects of systems operation needed to be thoroughly tested and the results incorporated into the flight operations manuals, this being a major requirement on the path to flight certification.

Chapter 5

Flight Testing and Certification

ANY NEW AIRCRAFT MUST BE tested in order to demonstrate that it can actually take to the air and, when airborne, perform flight in a safe and reliable manner. Once this has been established, further testing must be carried out to cover its area of intended use, whether military or civilian, passenger-carrying airliner or cargo carrier. In the case of the Concorde project, the challenge of supersonic flight was beyond the experience of its manufacturers and also, importantly, those regulatory authorities that would have to certify its fitness to carry airline passengers. Consequently, Concorde became the most tested airliner in history. New regulations were drawn up to cover possible eventualities that were hitherto undreamed of by the certification bodies of the partner countries.

The Flight Testing Programme

THE FLIGHT TEST PROGRAMME had several distinct phases, the first part being the development flying that would prove the design calculations, test the aircraft systems, and establish some

basic performance criteria. After initial subsonic handling tests, 'flutter' tests were carried out to check that any vibrations due to aerodynamic and structural interaction would not be amplified throughout the aircraft and result in catastrophic failure. Once this had been successfully accomplished, the flight envelope could be gradually expanded through the transonic phase of flight.

Later in the programme, the emphasis was placed on certification flying in which the aircraft was put through rigorous testing to meet the stringent requirements of the British and French airworthiness authorities, a necessary step before Concorde could enter airline service. Another phase of testing involved route-proving and endurance flights that could demonstrate the ability of the aircraft to carry out realistic, supersonic, airline operations.

RIGHT Pre-production
Concorde 101 G-AXDN
after roll-out at Filton,
January 1971

The Development Fleet

IN SUCH A RADICALLY DIFFERENT environment from that of the conventional subsonic airliner, there were many avenues to be explored before supersonic passenger flight could become reality. The design innovations in Concorde needed to be refined, and in some areas re-designed, before the relevant certification authorities would be sufficiently satisfied that this groundbreaking aircraft was fit to be granted its full passenger-carrying Certificate of Airworthiness (C of A). This momentous event was finally attained, late in 1975, after the development fleet had accumulated a combined total of 5,335 flying hours.

Originally, plans were made for a development fleet of seven aircraft but this was later reduced to a total of six, three from each country. The fleet initially consisted of the two prototypes, 001 (F-WTSS) and 002 (G-BSST), and the two pre-production aircraft, 101

RIGHT Pre-production
Concorde 101 G-AXDN
after roll-out at Filton,
January 1971

(G-AXDN) and 102 (F-WTSA). These latter two aircraft were sometimes referred to, incorrectly, as 01 and 02. Aircraft number 101 was the only British-built Concorde to have an 'odd' constructor's number, all others being evenly numbered. The first four air-

craft were, effectively, purely test aircraft and internally bore little resemblance to an airliner. Each prototype carried around 12 tons of test instrumentation that recorded measurements of pressure, temperature, acceleration, and attitude, onto magnetic tape while airborne for later analysis on the ground. Other data was transmitted in 'real time' while in flight, via telemetry, to ground monitoring stations.

These four dedicated test aircraft were later joined by two, so-called, 'production standard' aircraft, 201 (F-WTSB) and 202 (G-BBDG). As in the case of the prototypes, one pre-production, and one production standard Concorde, from each of the participating partners were allocated to the development programme.

Historic First Flights

THE FRENCH PROTOTYPE, DESIGnated 001 and registered F-WTSS, was ceremonially 'rolled out' at Toulouse on December 11 1967. After much programme slippage, it eventually made its maiden flight just over a year behind schedule, on March 2 1969, flown by test pilot Andre Turcat and crewmembers Jacques Guignard, Michel Retif, and Henri Perrier. The world's press covered this historic event and it was televised live, such was the interest the event had generated. This aircraft went on to complete 397 flights totalling 812 flying hours, of which 255 hours were at supersonic speeds, before being retired to the French Air Museum at Le Bourget airport, near Paris, on October 19 1973.

Having been rolled out at Filton on September 12 1968, the first British-built Concorde, 002, registered G-BSST, first flew on April 9 1969. Flown by test pilot Brian Trubshaw and crewed by co-pilot John Cochrane, and flight-test engineers Brian Watts, John Allen,

Mike Addley and Peter Holding, 002 landed at its flight test centre at RAF Fairford after a largely uneventful flight. One relatively minor difficulty was that both altimeters failed, leaving Trubshaw with the task of judging his immaculate touchdown by visual reference only. After a test programme of 438 flights, including 186 flights at supersonic speeds and amassing a total of 838 flying hours, 002 made its final flight to the Fleet Air Arm Museum, Yeovilton, on March 4 1976.

Supersonic At Last!

THE REALITY OF A SUPERSONIC airliner came a step closer when, on October 1 1969, Concorde 001 exceeded Mach 1, and then flew above that symbolic number for nine minutes, reaching a speed of Mach 1.5, equivalent to 1,125 miles per hour. The fact that this did not occur until flight number 45 in the flight test programme was an indication of the caution exercised throughout the whole of the Concorde test and development programme. In fact, it was not until March 25 1970 that the second aircraft followed suit, and achieved its first flight in excess of Mach 1. Pilots were generally agreed that this was a particularly good-mannered and precise aircraft to fly, coupled with excellent ground handling characteristics.

Such was the confidence shown in its qualities that, in November 1969, captains from four airlines were given the opportunity to fly Concorde. One pilot from Air France, BOAC, Pan American and TWA, was first given two sessions in the flight simulator at Toulouse prior to taking the controls of Concorde. Each of the four flew the aircraft at speeds of up to Mach 1.2 (850 miles per hour), after which they all concurred that the aircraft was easy to fly and should present no problems for the airline pilots and engineers when it was introduced into service.

Test flying progressed steadily with both 001 and 002 exceeding Mach 2 (1,350 miles per hour), within days of each other, in November 1970. The effects of sustained cruise at Mach 2 were virtually unknown as most military experience had been gained over much shorter time scales. Although many supersonic test flights were carried out largely over the sea, the need to provide close radar supervision within reach of rescue services over a route of some 800 miles necessitated the use of a supersonic 'overland' test route. This route ran from north to south along the western coasts of both Scotland and Wales, and over part of Cornwall. People living in these comparatively sparsely populated regions were the first to experience the signature 'double boom' made by Concorde; some were driven to formally protest to the authorities even though, in most cases, prior warning of test flights had been given.

Failure of one or more engines, and the consequences of controllability arising from such an incident, was investigated early in the testing at Mach 2 and above. First one engine, then a second on the same side of the aircraft were deliberately shut down without major effect to controllability, contrary to the forecasts of doubters. This was further demonstrated when, in January 1971, Concorde 001 suffered an engine

surge while travelling at supersonic speed. The surge caused part of the variable intake ramp to break loose, which was then ingested, causing damage that was contained within the engine. The aircraft returned safely to Toulouse on three engines, and made a normal landing.

Overseas Tours and Demonstration Flights

CONCORDE MADE ITS FIRST inter-continental flight when 001 flew from Toulouse to Dakar on May 25 1971, returning to Paris one day later for the opening day of the Paris Air Show. The Dakar to Paris leg, a distance of 2,500 miles, was flown in 2 hours 52 minutes, including 2 hours 7 minutes at supersonic speed. In September that same year, 001 flew to South America for a 15-day tour and visited Rio de Janeiro, Sao Paulo and Buenos Aires, demonstrating its ability to operate in the traffic patterns and climatic conditions of that region.

Not to be outdone, Concorde 002 left its Fairford test base in June 1972 for a, so-called, world tour that actually took it to Australia and back, via the Middle East and Far East. This tour covered a route of some 46,000 miles and was scheduled over 30 days, taking in most major cities including Athens, Tehran, Bahrain, Bombay (Mumbai), Bangkok, Singapore, Tokyo, Sydney and Melbourne. Returning to Heathrow on July 1st, the tour had shown that Concorde was capable of operating to airline schedules and, apart from a weather radar problem and an unserviceable valve in its air-conditioning system, proved largely trouble free. Aircraft of the test and development fleet carried out many further route proving and develop-ment flights, with much of this flying being accomplished by the two production-standard aircraft as these were more representative of the final airline version. Between them, Concorde 201 (F-WTSB) and Concorde 202 (G-BBDG) amassed a total of 2,192 flying hours.

Differences between Versions

AFTER A GESTATION PERIOD lasting around 13 years from concept to readiness for airline service, Concorde was, at the time, the most tested airliner in the history of flight. Its evolution from prototype to final airline production model had been gradual. Few casual observers could distinguish between the changes to the aircraft's outline, as the design was refined into the classic shape that was Concorde. Externally, the most notable difference between the prototypes and all of the later versions was in the shape of the droop nose and visor assemblies. On both prototypes, the visor had only two windows, whereas all later models had a six-pane glazing array that, together with a more slender nose profile, gave a much-improved view forward when the nose and visor were fully raised. Other, more subtle, changes were made to the contour of the wing, revisions were made to the engine intakes and exhaust nozzles and, from the first 'production standard' aircraft, the rear fuselage fairing was extended in length and given its distinctive upswept lower profile. The explosive-powered escape hatches that were fitted on the two prototypes for the emergency escape of the flight test crews were deleted, the retractable tail bumper skid was fitted with wheels, and there were differences in the cabin window arrangement. The ventral stairway and door at the rear of the cabin were deleted, and new passenger and cabin service doors were introduced at the rear galley area.

Further versions were planned including a dedicated freighter for the Fedex logistics company, and a passenger version known as the Concorde 'B' proposal. The Concorde 'B' was a longer-range variant with much improved fuel economy, refined aerodynamics that included droopable wing leading edge slats, for increased low speed lift, and lengthened wing tips. Noise was also to be reduced with modifications to the propulsion system that included replacing the low-pressure compressor by a compressor with increased diameter, and a new two-stage low-pressure turbine assembly, along with sound absorbing material in the intake and exhaust assemblies. Weight increase due to the aircraft changes was to be partly offset by the use of lighter carbon-fibre composite materials for the doors and some control surfaces. In the event, neither of these proposals was proceeded with.

The technical success of the Concorde project was the result of a unique collaboration that was a tribute to all those engineering, technical and flight test personnel of both Britain and France who were involved in it. All were enthusiastic in their determination to confound the doubters and produce a supersonic airliner that would remain in service for over 25 years. Speaking after his retirement, the late BAC Concorde chief test pilot, Brian Trubshaw, gave this testimony to their endeavours: "Concorde flies at a speed slightly faster than a rifle bullet and carries passengers of all ages. This remarkable aircraft is a lovely aeroplane to fly. It is a great and everlasting tribute to the British and French teams that created it. To fly the British-assembled prototype for the first time was the highlight of my flying career and I have always been extremely proud to be associated with Concorde."

BELOW British-built Concorde comes in for a perfect landing at Fairford Airfield, Gloucestershire, after her inaugural flight

Chapter 6

Concorde in Airline Service

IN THE EARLY YEARS OF THE 1970s, a press release made the following bold statement: "Soon there will be only two kinds of airliner: Concorde, and all the rest". While it is undoubtedly true that Concorde was dramatically different from all other airliners, and has always been regarded as something special, the

claim was almost certainly made in the hope that airlines would be falling over themselves in the rush to place orders for this, as yet, unproven aircraft. Even the opening word of the statement, "Soon", was somewhat optimistic, as it was several years before its entry into airline service was to be achieved. The introduction into airline service of any new aircraft type is fraught with difficulty, and delays are often the case. With Concorde, there were many problems to be overcome, not least those of protests against the sonic boom, as well as the specific technical and operational requirements associated with supersonic flight.

Nowhere was there any stronger protest than in the United States where, after pressure from its electors, Congress banned Concorde from landing anywhere within its territory. Without the prime transatlantic routes to the United States, there was little prospect of commercial viability for any supersonic airliner.

Changed Requirements and Cancelled Orders

PROSPECTIVE AIRLINE CUSTOMERS were involved in the Concorde project from the early years of the programme. Many sought greater payload capacity although this was at odds with some of the original design planning. In 1964 a seating layout for 118 passengers was proposed. The following year this was amended to provide a capacity for 139 seats, at a pitch of 34 inches, with a take-off weight of some 340,000 pounds. This version became known as the pre-production standard aircraft. It was substantially different from the prototypes in that the cabin was lengthened by just over 19 feet whereas the overall aircraft length increased by only 6ft 6in. This was achieved by moving the rear pressure bulkhead rearwards necessitating deletion of the rear ventral door which was replaced by two side access doors at the rear of the

LEFT F-BTSC in early Air France livery, circa 1975. This was the aircraft that crashed at Gonesse, near Paris, on July 25 2000 cabin, the left for passenger use, and the right for galley servicing.

This newer proposal was received favourably by some 16 airlines that, by mid-1967, had together placed a total of 74 options for purchase of this aircraft. In July 1972, BOAC and France signed firm orders for a total of nine aircraft, five for the British airline and four for the French. This milestone was hailed by Sir George Edwards, Chairman of BAC, as "…the end of the beginning…" of the Concorde project. Overseas sales hopes were anticipated on the back of sales to the two main American carriers, Pan American and TWA. However, both had undergone poor trading experiences in the period leading up to their option confirmation date and, in the light of their financial situation, began to doubt the operating benefits of Concorde, while the prospect of the additional burden of the aircraft costs began to weigh heavily. It was only around 18 months later that, to paraphrase the 1972 statement by Sir George Edwards, "…the beginning of the end…" was signalled. On January 31 1973, the date when both airlines' options to purchase were due to expire, both Pan American and TWA announced they would not proceed with their purchases. In a deteriorating world financial climate, in which oil prices had rocketed, other airlines rapidly followed suit, and also declined to confirm their orders. The crash of the TU-144 at the Paris Air Show added further to the air of gloom around the supersonic airliner industry.

By 1976, BOAC had merged along with British European Airways to become British Airways. This airline was bullish about the prospects of 'breaking even' on its proposed Concorde routes, based on a calculated average load factor of 55%. With this prospect, a somewhat optimistic one from the point of view

of the critics, its supporters eagerly anticipated Concorde's entry into airline service.

Racing Against a Jumbo

ON JUNE 13 1974, CONCORDE 02 flew to Boston Logan airport, Massachusetts, for the naming of the new international Terminal E. Its flight from Paris to Boston was made in a new record time of 3 hours 9 minutes. On June 17, Concorde 02 showed the world its timesaving capabilities in a spectacular, comparative demonstration. It took off from Boston at almost the same time as an Air France Boeing 747 took off from Paris, en route for Boston. The two aircraft crossed when the Boeing 747 was 620 miles outbound from Paris, and Concorde 02 was around 2,400 miles from Boston. After a turnround time at Paris of 68 minutes, 02 set off for its return flight to Boston, where it landed 11 minutes before the Boeing 747.

Scheduled Flights Begin

CONCORDE SCHEDULED FLIGHTS eventually began on January 21 1976: British Airways opened its London to Bahrain service, while Air France operated the first of its Paris to Rio de Janeiro flights. The following month, the US lifted the ban on Concorde landing on US territory. Any joy at the decision was short-lived as the New York authorities promptly initiated a local ban. This forced both British Airways and Air France to alter their original plans and both airlines commenced their respective services from London and Paris to Washington DC on May 24 1976.

It took until late in 1977 before the objections by New York were overcome, and regular services to Kennedy (JFK) airport in New York commenced on November 22 1977 from both Paris and London. These routes became the main focus of Concorde operations for the majority of its airline life. Briefly, in 1977, and between 1979-80, British Airways and Singapore Airlines oper-

ABOVE Passengers about to embark on a supersonic trip

ated a shared service between London and Singapore, via Bahrain. One BA aircraft, G-BOAD, was painted in Singapore Airways livery on its port side and British Airways livery on the starboard side. Due to complaints, on the grounds of noise, by the Malaysian government, the service was suspended until a new routing that bypassed Malaysian airspace had been designed. The Singapore services were eventually halted after India prevented supersonic flight over its territory, thus rendering the route no longer viable as a supersonic service.

Air France flew regular services to Mexico City, via Washington DC between late 1979 and November 1982. At various times, scheduled services were operated to Caracas, Venezuela, with a technical stop at Santa Maria, Azores, and to Rio de Janeiro via Dakar, in Senegal.

The Passenger Experience

THOSE WHO HAD BEEN PRIVI-
leged to fly in the First or Business Class
cabins on the wide-bodied airliners of
the time, and had become used to luxu-
ries such as fully reclining seats, lounge
areas and in-flight
movies, were faced
with a totally dif-
ferent experience
when flying on
Concorde. On both
British Airways and
Air France aircraft,
the passenger cab-
ins were configured
in a 'single' class
with around 90 to
100 seats, arranged
in pairs either side
of a central aisle. A
somewhat cramped
cabin, with aisle
headroom limited
to around six feet,
and legroom com-
parable to that of

standard coach class on other airliners
of the day, coupled with its relatively
narrow seats, gave little visible
indication of 'luxury' air travel to the
embarking passengers. Although
the fare price was the same for all, those
passengers seated in the forward section
of the cabin considered this area to be
somewhat more prestigious, and a little
quieter, than the rearmost area. This

BELOW Space was at a
premium, leading to
somewhat cramped
conditions in the galley

was seen by some as being a carryover from the First Class culture, wherein the premium seats were usually at the front of the aircraft.

The cabin windows were much smaller than on other airliners, their reduced size being partly due to the need to minimise the effects of any loss of cabin pressure at extreme altitude in the event of window failure. In the supersonic cruise the windows became warm to the touch but their somewhat restricted view allowed passengers to see the curvature of the earth on the horizon. In-flight video entertainment was restricted to the plasma display screen on each cabin forward bulkhead that showed a welcome message while passengers were boarding, and the altitude, outside air temperature, airspeed, and the Mach number, during the flight. This display became the focus of attention as the aircraft approached the magical Mach 1 and Mach 2 numbers, and was often used as the backdrop for souvenir photographs.

After landing, it displayed a 'Thank you for flying Concorde' message.

With the number of cabin crew being significantly less per passenger than that on wide bodied aircraft, and the number of lavatories being kept to a minimum due to space considerations, the passenger was justified in expecting something exceptional for his or her, not inconsiderable, ticket cost. The first obvious benefit was the scheduled journey time of less than half of that on a conventional airliner. This afforded the prospect of a same-day return journey from London to New York, an attractive proposition to the business traveller.

In compensation for the somewhat limited space and facilities, the emphasis was on service to the passenger. Every effort was made by cabin crew to give a truly 'first class' service. Food and drinks were of the best possible standard, surpassing that available on many high-end flights. British Airways meal service was on specially designed Wedgwood crockery of compact dimensions, with silver cutlery that was shorter than usual, again reflecting the space limitations on board. After the 9/11 events in 2001, the cutlery was replaced by plastic items, wrapped in a cloth napkin and presented in a brushed stainless steel napkin ring. Air France menu choices typically included champagne and caviar with a selection of hors d'oeuvres, a choice from three elegant main dishes, including vegetarian options, followed by a selection of cheeses, fruits and pastries.

The Braniff Affair

THE NOW DEFUNCT AMERICAN airline Braniff International had a brief flirtation with Concorde operations between 1979 and 1980. In a somewhat complex arrangement, Braniff leased Concordes from British Airways and Air France and, in doing so, became the only American airline to fly a supersonic aircraft. These were to be used on flights from Dallas-Fort Worth (DFW), in Texas, to feed into the scheduled services of their respective British and French owners from Washington DC and New York, to London and Paris. For legal reasons, the aircraft were registered in both the United States and their

registration N94AE), and Captain Ken Larson, at the controls of the Air France Concorde F-BVFC (N94FC), made simultaneous landings on parallel runways at DFW

countries of origin; a sticker covered the non-USA registration while Braniff operated the aircraft. The leased aircraft remained in their original liveries but were flown by Braniff flight crews on the return legs between DFW and New York or Washington. A pilot from the owner airline was usually present on the flight deck in order to satisfy the requirements of the aircraft insurance policy. Officially, all of the Braniff flights over the United States were subsonic but, on more than one occasion, the 'following wind' caused the aircraft to exceed the government-imposed limitation, and Concorde became supersonic for a short time.

On January 12 1979, Braniff International's Concorde services were opened in spectacular style when their pilots Captain Glenn Shoop, flying British Airways Concorde G-BOAE (US airport. The impact on the travelling public was less than spectacular: poorer than expected passenger bookings soon signalled the end of Braniff's brave attempt to establish itself as a successful operator of a supersonic airliner, albeit in subsonic mode. Overall, the load factors on the Braniff flights were usually less than 25% of capacity, particularly on the Dallas-Fort Worth to Washington service. This was partly due to the premium of 10% above the regular First Class price that the airline originally charged for the privilege of flying aboard Concorde. Even when the fares were reduced to parity with those of First Class, the load factors did not increase significantly. The airline eventually withdrew the Concorde services, the last such flight from DFW being made in June 1980 with only 60 passengers on board. Two years later, Braniff ceased operations.

Seasonal Schedules and Charter Flights

APART FROM THE MORE PUBLI-
cised transatlantic routes there were
winter-only scheduled Concorde flights
by British Airways to Barbados and,
around the festive season, the occasional
charter flight to Rovaniemi, Finland, the
home of Santa Claus. The more affluent
charter passenger could also fly around
the world on a series of global flights,
made by both British Airways and Air
France Concorde aircraft, organised by
companies such as Goodwood Travel,
American Express, Kuoni, Prado
Voyages, and Intrav. These flights were
flown over several days, to allow for
passenger sightseeing, but with a total
flight time averaging a little over 30
hours, around half of which was flown
at supersonic speed. Many world speed
records were established during these
epic journeys, some probably remaining
unbroken for many years to come.

For the less affluent, the opportunity
to fly supersonically became reality with
the introduction of the 'Trip around the
Bay' charters. Both Air France and
British Airways flew similar flights,
from various airports in
France and Britain that
comprised a round-trip,
including supersonic
travel, to the Bay of
Biscay. These flights
became extremely pop-
ular, particularly with
British enthusiasts and
first-time fliers alike, as
they enjoyed both the
supersonic experience,
and a taste of the luxury
that went with it.

LEFT F-BTSD in
promotional livery for
new Pepsi drinks can.
This aircraft was
selected as it was due
for a scheduled
maintenance outage
and repaint

Chapter 7

Concorde Facts and Figures

How Big, How Fast, How Many

THE FACTS AND FIGURES BELOW are taken from the British Airways publication issued to commemorate the period of airline service from 1976 to 2003 of the world's first supersonic airliner, 'Celebrating Concorde – the supersonic facts'.

Length:	203 feet 9 inches
Wingspan:	83 feet 8 inches
Height:	37 feet 1 inch
Fuselage width:	9 feet 6 inches
Take-off weight:	408,000 pounds maximum
Take-off speed:	250 miles per hour
Cruising speed:	1,350 miles per hour, Mach 2.0
Landing speed:	187 miles per hour
Cruising altitude:	Up to 60,000 feet
Range:	4,143 miles
Engines:	Four Rolls-Royce/SNECMA Olympus 593 turbojets
Engine power:	38,000 pounds thrust with reheat (each)
Fuel capacity:	26,286 imperial gallons
Fuel consumption:	5,638 imperial gallons per hour
Max payload:	100 passengers and 2.5 tonnes cargo
Cabin seating:	100: 40, front cabin and 60, rear cabin
Flight crew:	3: two pilots, 1 flight engineer
Cabin crew:	6

A Versatile Fuel System

THE FUEL SYSTEM IN CONCORDE was designed to play a major part in the overall operation of the aircraft. Apart from its primary purpose of storing fuel and supplying it to the engines, fuel was also used as a heat sink for the purpose of removing excess heat from the air conditioning system, hydraulic system and engine oil systems, through heat exchangers, to the fuel. One of the most important factors in supersonic flight is the requirement to reduce drag to a minimum, both for reasons of performance and economy. To avoid increased drag that would arise when trimming the aircraft using conventional trim tabs or a variable-incidence tail-plane, the Concorde fuel system was used to adjust the trim of the aircraft in response to the requirements of each phase of flight.

Apart from the fuel storage and engine supply fuel tanks there are a further three transfer and reserve tanks, two located in a symmetrical pair, one in each wing, and the third located in the rear fuselage. These transfer and

reserve tanks hold around one-third of the total fuel capacity of the aircraft. In supersonic flight, the aerodynamic centre of lift shifted rearward by around 6 feet from its subsonic datum. In designing Concorde, the conventional tail-plane was discarded in favour of a fuel transfer system that could effectively move the aircraft centre of

LEFT Concorde touching down at Heathrow

gravity rearward, to compensate for the rearward shift in the aerodynamic centre of lift, during acceleration to supersonic speed. Before take-off, and during acceleration to Mach 2, fuel is progressively pumped out of the forward wing transfer tanks and transferred to the rear fuselage transfer tank. Usually, around 20 tons of fuel were moved in order to obtain the requisite rearward shift of the centre of gravity. Toward the end of supersonic cruise, during deceleration, the reverse process was carried out to move the fuel forward to shift the centre of gravity forward again.

The ability to transfer fuel fore and aft also provided additional benefits at

lower speeds. With the centre of gravity rearwards during take-off and landing, the control surfaces on the trailing edges of the wings, known as elevons, were drooped slightly downwards to counteract the 'tail-heavy' condition. In so doing, this effectively increased the camber of the wing, and thus generated additional lift at lower speeds. With the

ability to also transfer fuel from one side of the aircraft to the other, lateral trim could again be achieved without the need for any control surface deflection that would otherwise have increased drag and reduced performance.

Fuel transfer was carried out by the flight engineer from his control panel on the right hand side of the flight deck, behind the co-pilot. This panel provided the facility for fuel to be transferred automatically, and then stopped, when the required amount of fuel had been moved between tanks. Dynamic marker 'bugs' on the airspeed indicators and mach meters, on both of their main instrument panels, kept the pilots informed of the current aircraft centre of gravity. The bugs also gave real-time indications of the speed that could be flown for the current centre of gravity position.

Did You Know?

DURING SUPERSONIC FLIGHT THE fuselage stretched between six and ten inches due to the heat generated by air friction. Concorde was painted, predominantly, in a special white coating that was developed to both accommodate the stretching of the fuselage, and also assist in heat dissipation. At Mach 2, aircraft skin temperatures reached as high as 127°C on the tip of the nose, and 105°C on the wing leading edges. Even the rear cabin outer skin temperature reached around 91°C. During each

flight, the airframe was subjected to two distinct cooling and heating cycles, compared to the single cooling and 'warming' cycle of a conventional airliner. As Concorde climbed into the colder air at altitude, the airframe cooled. As it accelerated to supersonic speed, the airframe became heated to temperatures in excess of 100°C. During the deceleration, while still in colder air at high altitude, it first cooled, and then gradually warmed to ambient temperature, as it descended further, prior to landing.

Relative to aircraft length, the wingspan of 83 feet 8 inches is much less than a conventional airliner. The main reason for this is due to the fact that Concorde used a particular aerodynamic phenomenon, known as vortex lift which gave the aircraft its exceptional performance. At the lower end of the speed range, its delta-shaped wings caused low-pressure vortices to form over the leading edges and upper wing surfaces, and thus maintain lift at high angles of attack. These vortices generated the familiar vapour cloud that was often seen around the wings of Concorde during take-off and landing. One disadvantage of the vortex effect

RIGHT Air France flight
crew at work

was that it caused light buffeting during initial climb-out, and throughout the approach to landing.

A striking feature of Concorde is its nose and visor arrangement. Except when parked, few have seen the aircraft, in close-up, with its nose and visor in the supersonic cruise position. This is largely due to the fact that the nose and visor are configured in a number of different positions according to the phase of flight or ground manoeuvring situation. When parked, both the nose and visor are in their 'fully up' positions, ie visor raised, and the nose at the 0° non-drooped position. For taxying and take-off, the visor was lowered, and the nose drooped to the 5° position. In subsonic cruise, the nose was raised to the non-drooped 0° position but the visor was left in the down position, provided the speed was less than 325 knots (Mach 0.8). Above that speed, and for supersonic cruise, the visor was fully raised. After deceleration to subsonic speed, and in the descent at speeds below 325 knots, the visor lowered and the nose was initially left at 0°, then lowered to 5°. For approach and landing, the visor was down, and the nose fully-drooped to the 12.5° position, provided the altitude

was less than 20,000 feet, and the speed below 270 knots. This additional amount of droop was necessary to provide forward vision for the pilots during the approach and landing phases of flight, where Concorde adopted

its trademark 'nose-high' attitude.

Take-off speed was around 220 knots (250 miles per hour), a considerable increase over, typically, the 165 knots (180 miles per hour) of a conventional airliner. Official cruise speed was Mach 2.04 (1,350 miles per hour), equivalent to twice the speed of sound at sea level. This speed has often been likened to being 'faster than a rifle bullet'. Flying at an altitude of up to 60,000 feet a typical journey time between London and New

York took a little under three and a half hours, against that of over seven and a half hours for a conventional airliner. This considerable time saving meant that, for a westward crossing of the Atlantic, the passenger could arrive in New York at a local time that was earlier than that at which they had left London, thanks to the time-zone change en route. This led to Concorde being dubbed 'faster than the sun' or, 'the time machine'.

In order to stop the aircraft after landing or, crucially, on an aborted take-off from around 171 knots (190mph), special carbon-compound brakes were developed that could bring Concorde to a standstill within one mile, at a total aircraft weight of around 408,000 pounds or 182 tons. The braking system was one of the first on a civilian airliner to use the anti-lock principle that prevented the wheels from locking when maximum braking effort was applied, and thus provided greater retardation.

Concorde was powered by four Bristol Siddeley (later, Rolls Royce)/ SNECMA Olympus 593 turbojets, each producing more than 38,000 pounds of thrust with reheat (after-burning). With reheat, fuel is injected into the exhaust gas stream after the turbine section of the engine, to produce additional power during take-off, and for the acceleration into supersonic flight. Pure turbo-jet engines were chosen because the requirements for supersonic flight were for an engine to have both a low bypass ratio and small frontal cross-section.

Although the engines produced sufficient power for the aircraft to achieve supersonic flight without using reheat, it was discovered during flight tests that more fuel was used in the non-reheated condition, due to the increased time taken during acceleration/transition from the subsonic cruise. Somewhat perversely, reheat was used for reasons of fuel economy, even though it is inherently less fuel efficient, because the quantity of fuel used for the acceleration to supersonic speed was actually less than that used in a non-reheated acceleration. For taxying after landing, the two inboard engines were shut down to conserve fuel. As turbo-jet engines can only operate efficiently at subsonic speeds, the air intake system was designed to modify the airflow such that, at Mach 2, the velocity of air entering the engine was reduced to around Mach 0.5.

Supersonic Travel Trivia

IN SUPERSONIC FLIGHT, CONCORDE travelled more than twice as fast as conventional aircraft. When flying in the same direction, those other aircraft appeared to be flying backwards.

Concorde had quite small passenger windows. At the extremely high altitude that Concorde flew, a broken window would have caused rapid decompression, leading to the passengers and crew passing out before the aircraft could be brought down to a safe altitude. Oxygen masks alone would not provide sufficient margin for survival; therefore, the windows were made smaller to maintain sufficient cabin pressure during the descent.

More than 2.5 million passengers have flown supersonically on British Airways Concorde aircraft. Fuel consumption, per passenger, averaged around 14 miles per gallon.

Because Concorde flew westward faster than the rotation of the Earth, it was possible to take off from London just after sunset, and see the sun rise in the west, en route to the USA.

When Concorde flew eastward the weight of everyone onboard was temporarily reduced by about 1%. This was due to the centrifugal effect created by its supersonic airspeed being added to the opposing rotational speed of the Earth. Flying westward, the weight of those onboard remained virtually unchanged due to the co-directional rotation of the Earth. At its maximum altitude, a person's weight was reduced by around 0.6% caused by the increased distance from the centre of Earth.

During the televised Live Aid famine relief concerts held on July 13 1985, the singer Phil Collins was able to perform at venues in London and Philadelphia, USA, on the same day, flying between the two cities on Concorde.

Concorde increased in length by up to 10 inches during supersonic flight due to kinetic heating.

In November 1986, a BA Concorde flew around the world, covering 28,238 miles in 29 hours and 39 minutes.

BA Concorde G-BOAD flew the fastest transatlantic passenger flight from New York to London on February 7 1996, in 2 hours, 52 minutes and 59 seconds.

RIGHT The impressive power of Concorde, shortly after departure from Heathrow

Concorde's oldest passenger was 105-year-old Eva Woodman, from Bristol, who enjoyed a 90-minute supersonic flight from Filton, around the Bay of Biscay in May 1998.

One Concorde passenger, Justin Cornell, a bank clerk from Portsmouth, flew to New York after purchasing 900

packets of chocolate biscuits, at a cost of £800, in a special promotion in his local Tesco supermarket. The extra loyalty points on his club card were converted into Air Miles, which were also part of a special bonus promotion that enabled him to accumulate sufficient miles for the Concorde trip. His one fear was that his weight of 23 stones would prevent him from making the trip, but he was fortunately able to make the journey of a lifetime. His flight took place shortly after the return to service of Concorde, following the Paris crash, and was carrying only 12 passengers at the time. On returning, he took a weight-reduction course, and subsequently lost over 10 stones in weight. Not to be tempted by his purchase, the biscuits were sold, and the proceeds donated to charity. His eye for a bargain had previously been successful with a first class flight to San Francisco, albeit in a subsonic aircraft, after spending some £300 on shampoo in another sales promotion at a supermarket.

In a BBC poll, carried out in March 2006 in connection with the programme Great British Design Quest, in which the public were asked to vote on their favourite design icon since

1900, Concorde was declared the winner. In doing so, it beat another classic aircraft, the Spitfire, which was placed third, after the map of the London Underground that was in second place.

The Concorde 'B' Proposal

IN THE MID-1970S, THE MANU-facturers Aerospatiale and BAC issued a proposal for an improved version of Concorde known as the Concorde 'B' version. This model would have enabled the expansion of the supersonic route structure due to its increased design-range of around 4,079 miles, compared to the 3,690 miles of the standard version. This would have allowed single sector operations to the eastern coastal cities of the United States from most European capitals, from the United States to Japan in two sectors and from Europe to Australia in three sectors. Although the aircraft weight would be greater, this would have been offset by improvements in fuel efficiency. As the range of the standard Concorde was eventually increased to around 4,500 miles through comparatively small design refinements, the potential for the 'B' version offered even greater possibilities. Noise was to be substantially lower than the original model, due to radical design changes in the engines coupled with improved aerodynamics that would improve lift at lower speeds and thus reduce the engine thrust required at take-off and landing. The take-off noise was to be reduced from 119.5db to around 109db, and at landing from 116.7db to 109db.

The planned engine modifications entailed increasing the diameter of the low-pressure compressor, and replacing the single-stage low-pressure turbine with a two-stage unit. The air flow through the modified engine was calculated to be 25% greater on take-off, and 35% greater on approach to landing than the existing engine, and the corresponding increase in thrust throughout the entire flight envelope being sufficient to enable the removal of the reheat system. Aerodynamic changes were to include leading-edge slats to improve lift, and thereby allow a reduced angle of attack at low speed,

optimised camber and twist of the wing to improve lift and smoothness at Mach 2, and lengthened wing tips.

The Concorde 'B' modifications were planned to be introduced from the seventeenth aircraft onwards: in the event, the proposal was dropped when the decision was made to cease production after Concorde 216 had been completed.

Chapter 8

The Twilight Years

The Cost/ Benefit Imbalance

THE ECONOMICS OF THE Concorde programme were under continual scrutiny on both sides of the English Channel. The development costs alone had been around £1.134 billion, funded in equal shares by Britain and France. Failure of airlines to take up their options to purchase caused an inordinate increase in the unit production costs for the 16 aircraft that eventually emerged from the production lines at Filton and Toulouse. The actual production cost for these 16 aircraft was around £654 million with only £278 million recovered in sales receipts. Together with the rising price of fuel that was unforeseen when the programme was initiated, the partner governments had, by the mid-1980s, become mutually concerned over the continuing financial burden. With no further prospect of orders for Concorde, the British government decided to withdraw funding to Rolls-Royce and

British Aerospace (formerly, BAC). Concorde operations had failed to become self-financing and, without government support, the future of the supersonic airliner was in doubt.

Technical Tribulations

DURING THE IN-SERVICE LIFE OF Concorde there were comparatively few major technical problems for an aircraft of its type, operating as it did in a flight environment that was a departure from previous airline experience. Needless to say, because of the controversy that surrounded all areas of Concorde operations on technical, cost, or environmental issues, any technical problems that arose were highlighted by its opponents, and often featured in the media. One aspect that was a recurring problem for the Concorde design and engineering staffs was the incidence of several rudder failures during the period 1989 to 1992. These involved the loss of part of a rudder section during flight that was usually signalled by

LEFT Retracting her landing gear after take-off

vibration, particularly at supersonic speed. The problem necessitated an expensive re-design and manufacturing process, prior to the replacement of all rudders in the Concorde fleet. This action proved largely successful, although at least one further rudder separation occurred, in 1998, and the separation of a large portion of an elevon control surface from the aircraft wing, during its climb to cruising altitude, earlier in the same year.

Various engine problems had been experienced at times throughout Concorde's service life, including surging, failure of reverse thrust components, low oil pressure, and secondary damage caused by foreign objects. Most of the technical failures were typical for almost any aircraft in airline operation and were not purely 'supersonic' problems. One recurring problem, however, was to have a significant impact on Concorde operations and was,

ultimately, to hasten its demise. During the life of Concorde in airline service there were a total of 60 known tyre failures, of which seven caused damage to fuel tanks.

In June 1979, an Air France Concorde, F-BVFC, had to return to that airport after two main tyres blew out during take-off from Washington DC. Electrical wiring, and some of the wing structure, was damaged after being struck by debris from the tyres. Fuel and hydraulic leakage also occurred. The following month, at the same airport, another Air France Concorde F-BVFD also blew a tyre during take-off and, subsequently, during the climb, incurred a compressor stall that was

RIGHT Grounded Concorde at Heathrow

probably caused by foreign object ingestion. In September 1980, again at Washington, British Airways Concorde G-BOAF had a tyre burst on take-off that caused damage to an engine and part of the airframe. Another tyre burst during take-off from Washington, this time causing Air France Concorde F-BTSD to divert to New York's JFK airport, after vibration caused by foreign object damage led to an engine being shut down, took place in February 1981.

Further instances of tyre failure arose in July 1993, when G-BOAF blew a tyre during the landing roll at London Heathrow that was caused by brake seizure, the debris damaging the Number 3 engine, some wing structure, and part of the hydraulic system. In October of that year, another British Airways Concorde burst a tyre at Heathrow, while taxying for take-off, after a brake locked. On this occasion, a fuel tank was punctured by debris. Seven years later, this pattern of events was to be repeated, this time with tragic consequences, on a Tuesday afternoon, near Paris.

The Paris Accident

ON JULY 25 2000, AIR FRANCE Concorde F-BTSC commenced its take-off from Paris-Charles de Gaulle airport, carrying a full complement of passengers on a charter flight to New York. Shortly before rotation into take-off attitude, the aircraft ran over a strip

ABOVE The tyres being checked by BA personnel

engines producing thrust, the crew tried to raise the undercarriage, to reduce drag, but this failed to retract. The crew informed air traffic control that they were heading for the nearest airport, Le Bourget, but at only 200 feet altitude and with an airspeed of around 200 knots, the crew were faced with an impossible task when the Number 1 engine also lost thrust. The aircraft pitched up, and its angle of bank increased rapidly. The aircraft then crashed onto a hotel at Gonesse, with the loss of all of its 100 passengers, nine crew members, and four persons at the hotel. Less than one minute and thirty seconds had elapsed between the aircraft running over the metal strip, and the subsequent crash.

of metal that had fallen from another aircraft. This burst the front right tyre on the left landing gear bogie, throwing debris against the underside of the wing, causing the Number 5 fuel tank to rupture. As the aircraft continued its take-off, a major fire started under the left wing, and problems also occurred with the two left engines, particularly on the Number 2 engine that was indicating a fire alarm, and was then shut down by the crew as it was only producing near-idle power. At low altitude, on fire, and with only three

The immediate aftermath of the accident led to British Airways cancelling its two Concorde flights scheduled for later that day, but resumed services on the following day. Air France grounded its remaining five Concorde aircraft indefinitely, pending the outcome of the crash investigation. One of their aircraft, F-BVFC, was stranded in New York where it remained until special authorisation was obtained for it to fly back to Paris with no passengers, on September 21. British Airways continued to operate their Concorde fleet until, on the advice of the regulatory bodies, they withdrew them from service on August 15 2000. The following day, the Concorde certificate of airworthiness was withdrawn, effectively grounding all of the remaining fleet. A British Airways flight to New York was cancelled while the aircraft was taxying to the runway. The return flight aircraft, which was already at New York JFK airport, was given dispensation by the British CAA to be flown back to London without its passengers.

Towards the Return to Flight

THE METAL STRIP ON THE RUNway that burst the tyre had caused a portion of tread to be detached from the tyre casing. During certification of Concorde, such an eventuality had been foreseen and tests had been carried out that showed the aircraft fuel tanks could withstand the effects of a detached tread section measuring around 12 by 12 inches. In the accident, a piece of tread measuring over three times that size in

BELOW Back in the air again, 2001

length, and weighing around 10 pounds, had been sliced from the tyre. This had been propelled at high velocity, striking the underside of the aircraft's left wing, causing a hydraulic ripple effect in the fuel that caused the fuel tank to rupture with disastrous consequences.

Frustrated to a large extent by the slowness of both the French legal system and the investigating committee's

deliberations, it was decided to make a start on seeking ways to overcome the known technical shortcomings that had contributed to the accident. A working group was set up with representatives from British Airways, Air France, and the two aircraft manufacturers, to seek a solution to the problems of tyre bursts, undercarriage failure to retract, and engine surges. They were also tasked to implement fuel tank safety measures, all

with the one objective, that being the return of Concorde to airline service. By November 2000, the working group proposed the fitting of kevlar liners to the vulnerable fuel tanks, and the use of new tyres with greater resistance to damage that would, in the event of a burst, break into smaller fragments that would cause less damage. This work would cost around £1.5 million per aircraft to implement. British Airways was prepared to underwrite this sum on their fleet, as well as spending more money to upgrade the cabin interiors of their fleet before individual aircraft returned to service. It was a gamble that needed to be taken as the airlines were losing money, and prestige, while the Concorde fleet was grounded.

Cabin upgrade proposals were intended to brighten the interior with new lighting arrangements that would change colour to a cool blue as the aircraft accelerated through Mach 1. New, more comfortable, blue Connolly-leather seats were made from technologically advanced materials that saved 20% of the original seat weight, affording potential fuel savings of around £1 million per year. The lavatories were also to be given a new,

more spacious feel with back-lit wall panels and new sanitary fittings. In the event, only the new seats and carpets were fitted at this stage, due to the pressure of work in satisfying the safety requirements.

British Airways fitted the first set of kevlar fuel tank liners to G-BOAF early in 2001, while Air France Concorde F-BVFB set off for the flight test centre at Istres, in southern France. Here, it undertook a number of flights fitted with a coloured-water, leak-simulation test rig that would show engineers how leaks of various magnitudes would behave at take-off speeds, and beyond. In April 2001, Air France obtained clearance from the French airworthiness authority to fly F-BTSD to Istres for tests on the new Michelin Near Zero Growth (NZG) tyres. In Britain, both Rolls-Royce and British Aerospace engineers carried out tests to determine engine behaviour and surge patterns at various simulated fuel leak rates. On June 19 2001, G-BOAF was rolled out from the British Airways maintenance hangar at London Heathrow, ready to undergo the necessary ground and flight testing prior to re-certification being granted by the British CAA.

After some taxying tests at Heathrow, G-BOAF was finally ready for the first of a series of verification flights, with a CAA test pilot as a crew member, which commenced on July 17 2001. Three days later, it returned to Heathrow having successfully completed its verification flights. By August 7 2001, the first British Airways Concorde departed Heathrow for Shannon, Ireland, for a period of crew training. Prior to this, all Concorde flight crews underwent an intense flight simulator course in preparation for the forthcoming Ireland trip. By late August, both airlines eagerly anticipated the result of their applications for the aircraft Certificate of Airworthiness to be granted but were frustrated by the regulatory authorities.

This waiting period was used to prepare G-BOAF for the re-marketed Concorde operations by a visit to the paint shop, from where it emerged as the first in the fleet to carry the new British Airways livery. The French were running a little behind the British with their fleet modification programme but making steady progress. Finally, on September 5 2001, the British CAA and French DGAC informed the airline companies, and the world's press, that Concorde was certified to return to service and could, once again, carry passengers. On September 11 2001, G-BOAF carried a full load of British Airways staff, as passengers, for a simulated airline sector flight. After a successful flight and landing, those on board were given the terrible news of the terrorist atrocity in New York, on the date forever known as 9/11.

The Beginning of the End

IN THE WAKE OF THE EVENTS OF 9/11, the airlines continued the modifications needed to ready Concorde for passenger flights. The negative effect on passengers' attitude towards air travel was causing concern as both airlines prepared for the resumption of scheduled services. On November 7 2001, Air France Concorde F-BTSD took off from Paris to re-commence scheduled flights to New York, followed some 45 minutes later by the British Airways flight to New York from Heathrow, flown by Concorde G-BOAE.

Later that day, G-BOAF took off on a British government charter to fly the Prime Minister to Washington DC for urgent discussions with the US President on the post-9/11 situation.

Although Concorde was still popular with those who could afford to fly on her, the transatlantic airline business, generally, was going through a poor trading in the aftermath of the terrorist attacks in New York. In April 2003, both Air France and British Airways made their announcements that they would cease Concorde operations later in the year. Their reasons for this action were given as poor passenger confidence following the Paris crash, lower than economical passenger numbers following the 9/11 incidents, and rising fuel and maintenance costs.

Chapter 9

Farewells and Finals

IN THE PERIOD FOLLOWING THE Paris accident and the subsequent events in New York on 9/11, the airline industry underwent a period of uncertainty. This was especially true with regard to the high-end passenger market where the lack of confidence in air travel, due to the threat of terrorism, coupled with rising costs in fuel and aircraft maintenance, resulted in poor returns for the airlines. The downturn in premium-fare passenger numbers was also partly attributed to the failures of some of the companies that had joined in the 'dot.com' revolution, and were now subject to the harsh reality of the global trading climate.

British Airways had made substantial losses on Concorde during the early 1980s. However, in the aftermath of the withdrawal by the British government of financial support for the Concorde programme, the airline had actually operated the aircraft at a profit. This had been helped when the loan made to the airline by the government, to purchase the supersonic fleet, was written off on privatisation of the airline in 1987. It had been suggested that annual profits as high as £50 million in the best year had been made: the finances were never open to full scrutiny but it was estimated that British Airways' total revenue income on the Concorde services was in the region of £1.75 billion. This was set

ABOVE The distinctive profile of Concorde, in flight and on the ground

against an estimated cost-base of around £1 billion for those services. Some of the profits were the result of a somewhat cynical pricing policy that saw a gradual increase in fares on Concorde, that were raised to match the perceived higher cost expectations of its wealthier passengers.

It has been claimed that Air France has never made an operating profit on its Concorde services. Until the airline was partly privatised in 1999, the government of France, who financed its operations, both supersonic and conventional, effectively owned it. One noticeable feature of Air France's Concorde operations that had a significant effect on its profitability was the substantially lower utilisation by the French airline when compared to that of British Airways. On average, the utilisation rate, in terms of total aircraft hours flown in airline service with Air France, was less than two-thirds of that

of British Airways. With a smaller fleet than that of the British airline, the scales weighed heavily against the French, especially as they had grounded one of their aircraft, Concorde 211, registration F-BVFD, as early as 1982. The Paris accident reduced their fleet still further. With reported load factors of around 40%, Concorde was not commercially viable for Air France.

The Decision is Taken

ON APRIL 10 2003, BRITISH AIRWAYS and Air France made simultaneous announcements that they would be retiring all their Concorde aircraft from service later that year. The reasons given were the reduction in passengers following the Paris accident, the adverse effect on transatlantic air travel following the 9/11 attacks, rising fuel prices, and increasing maintenance costs particularly those resulting from the ageing of the airframes. The decision to write off a substantial investment in returning Concorde to service was made against the backdrop of perceived greater losses that would be incurred should the premium-passenger market fail to improve. All those who flew, or had flown, in Concorde greeted the news with dismay, as did her crews and, in particular, her adoring public. She was, after all, the people's aircraft: not just an airliner, but a 'supersonic' airliner that had also become a symbol of international collaboration that was reflected in her name, Concorde.

The chairman of Air France, Jean-Cyril Spinetta said: "Air France deeply regrets having to make the decision to stop its Concorde operations, but it has become a necessity." He then announced that Air France would cease Concorde operations on May 31 2003. A British Airways spokesperson, Sara John, said the retirement of their supersonic service "…will be permanent as of October this year." The airline also declared its intention to 'Celebrate Concorde' during the final months in service, and also to give as many people as possible the opportunity to fly in the aircraft before its retirement.

On that same day, the chairman of Virgin Atlantic, Sir Richard Branson, offered to buy the British Airways Concorde fleet for his airline but this, and subsequent proposals made during the following months, were turned down. The aircraft manufacturers also made it clear that they were unwilling to provide the necessary ongoing technical and spares support.

Another reason that had been suggested, not given by the airlines, for Concorde being withdrawn was the belief that most of its premium-class passengers would remain loyal to the respective airlines, and thus would provide greater revenue if they were carried on the existing, more economical subsonic aircraft.

Au Revoir Concorde

AS HAD BEEN PREVIOUSLY announced, Air France became the first of the two airlines to cease Concorde flights. After more than 27 years in airline service, their final commercial flight ended when F-BTSD touched down at Paris-Charles de Gaulle airport, after flying from New York-JFK, on Saturday May 31 2003. Somewhat surprisingly, there were only 68 passengers on board, along with 11 crew members. Thus ended a glorious, if controversial, period in French aviation history. Since the first revenue-earning flight from Paris to Rio de Janeiro, via Dakar, on January 21 1976, Concorde had flown over 1.3 million passengers. After the resumption of Concorde flights in November 2001, Air France had carried over 40,000 passengers between Paris

and New York. Jean-Cyril Spinetta, chairman of Air France, said "This marks the end of an era for Air France and for the aviation world as a whole. Yet for all that, Concorde will never really stop flying, because it will always have a place in people's imagination".

Although this was the last scheduled flight, it was not the final Air France flight by Concorde. In the following few days there was a round-trip charter flight from Paris to the Bay of Biscay and, on June 2/3 2003, Air France flew a farewell round-trip Paris to New York flight, for its airline staff and employees, in F-BTSD. The last flight ever by an Air France Concorde took place on June 27 2003 when F-BVFC flew into retirement at Toulouse, where it was built.

The Long Goodbye

THE DEMISE OF THE BRITISH Airways Concorde fleet was in stark contrast to the relatively low-key events in France. In the final months of service, the aircraft was kept busy in not only its usual scheduled role, but also on a series of specially organised farewell flights. The final departure from Grantley Adams airport in Barbados took place on August 30 2003. By October, the series of farewell flights gained rapid momentum with a number of flights to North America. First was a visit by G-BOAG to Toronto on October 1 2003, followed on October 8 by G-BOAD when it called at Boston, setting a new east to west transatlantic record flight time from London Heathrow of 3 hours, 5 minutes and 34 seconds. Washington DC was the destination for G-BOAG on October 14.

BELOW Air France staff and crew pose beside Concorde after the last transatlantic flight

Late October saw a week of farewell flights around the United Kingdom. Visiting Birmingham, Belfast, Manchester, Cardiff and Edinburgh between October 20 and 24 2003, the flights carried over 350 special guests, and another 650 who had won competitions for their flight tickets. In a rare event, two Concorde aircraft landed simultaneously on parallel runways at London Heathrow, one an Edinburgh special flight and the other, a scheduled flight from New York.

The last commercial Concorde departure from Heathrow took place in the evening of October 23 2003.

Shortly after its westbound departure it flew over Windsor Castle, which had, by consent of Queen Elizabeth, been floodlit for the occasion, an honour normally reserved only for major state events. This aircraft, G-BOAG, left New York the following day on its final passenger flight from JFK airport, where it received a traditional farewell salute in the form of water, sprayed in a triumphal arch, by the airport fire authority.

British Airways formally retired its Concorde fleet on October 24 2003. Two aircraft flew round-trip sorties; G-BOAE made a return flight to Edinburgh, while G-BOAF took a party of VIP guests around the Bay of Biscay. As these two flights returned to London, they were joined by the last supersonic passenger flight from New York, and all three landed in sequence, at Heathrow, shortly after 4pm. The three aircraft then taxied around the airport for 45 minutes, seemingly to prolong the life of Concorde, before disembarking their passengers.

One month later, on November 26 2003, the final flight ever by a British Airways Concorde took place. Piloted by Captain Les Brodie, G-BOAF took

ABOVE Concorde in the sunset of her career

off from Heathrow for a supersonic flight around the Bay of Biscay. Carrying a group of VIP passengers, including Prince Andrew, Duke of York, the flight returned to Bristol, the city that had built Concorde. A large crowd had gathered at Filton airfield to witness this momentous event. Heavy skies and rain showers failed to drive them from their vantage points. Entertained by local radio stations, and a flying display by a Rolls-Royce-owned Spitfire, they patiently awaited their first sighting of the arriving Concorde. As G-BOAF approached the city, it first overflew the Clifton Suspension Bridge, where another large crowd had gathered, before commencing its long downwind leg toward the east. The crowd waited expectantly as the familiar, graceful shape came into view on its approach to Runway 27, where Concorde made her final touchdown, shortly after 1pm. The era of the supersonic airliner had ended.

Chapter 10

Preservation and Display

BEFORE THE FINAL WITHDRAWAL of Concorde from commercial services, there was much speculation as to the eventual fate of these historic and iconic airliners. Both of the airlines that operated her made similar announcements regarding the subsequent fate of their aircraft. Air France made it known before their last revenue-earning flight that it "…wished to allow as many people as possible to see this legendary aircraft, which has made its mark not just on Air France, but on aviation history. Air France is therefore paying homage to Concorde, which, displayed on these sites, will live on forever." It was announced that four of their aircraft would be donated to four major aviation institutions, with their fifth, and sole remaining, Concorde being scheduled for display at Paris-Charles de Gaulle airport.

The situation regarding the British Airways fleet was not so clear cut. The final decision on where the British airline's Concorde aircraft were to be located was not announced until October 30 2003. In making his announcement of the successful applicants, the airline's chief executive, Rod Eddington, said: "Since we announced the retirement of Concorde we have received a wide variety of interesting proposals from organisations wanting to give the aircraft permanent homes. We have chosen the final homes based on a number of criteria: their ability to properly exhibit and preserve the aircraft, their geographical location and accessibility to the public. We are working closely with each of the new homes to make sure they show off each Concorde at her best."

British Airways also stated that they had carried out a feasibility study into the possibility of maintaining one

BELOW Taxying for take-off at New York, JFK

Concorde in a flyable condition, so that it could be used on special, non-passenger carrying events. After discussions with the manufacturers, it had been decided that the cost of such a project was prohibitively expensive, and would not be pursued.

Those in the community that were to benefit from the Concorde withdrawal from service were disabled children and young people. In December 2003,

an auction of Concorde parts and memorabilia was held at London Olympia. The sale raised around £750,000 of which £500,000 was donated to the charity 'Get Kids Going!' that aims to give many disabled youngsters the opportunity to participate in sport. Among the items sold were a Mach meter, pilot and passenger seats, a nose cone, cutlery and blankets.

Concorde Retirement Locations

CONCORDE 001 F-WTSS – THE first prototype is preserved in the French Air and Space Museum, Le Bourget, Paris. This aircraft was the first Concorde to fly when she made her maiden flight on March 2 1969 at Toulouse, France, piloted by Andre Turcat.

Total number of flights: 397 (including 249 supersonic)
Hours flown: 812 hrs 19 min (including 254 hrs 49 min supersonic)

CONCORDE 002 G-BSST – THE second prototype and the first British-built aircraft to fly. Taking off from Filton, Bristol, on April 9 1969 with Brian Trubshaw at the controls, she landed at the flight test centre at RAF Fairford. Purchased in 1976 for the nation, by the Science Museum, London, this aircraft is preserved and on display to the public in the Leading Edge Hall at the Fleet Air Arm Museum, Yeovilton, Somerset.

Total number of flights: 438 (196 supersonic)
Hours flown: 836 hrs 9 min (173 hrs 26 min supersonic)

CONCORDE 101 G-AXDN – THE British pre-production aircraft (also referred to as 01). First flown on December 17 1971, this aircraft is owned by the Duxford Aviation Society and is on display at the Imperial War Museum's Air Space exhibition centre at Duxford, Cambridgeshire.

Total number of flights: 273 (168 supersonic)
Hours flown: 574 hrs 49 min (387 hrs supersonic)

CONCORDE 102 F-WTSA – ALSO known as 02. The French pre-production aircraft first flew on January 10 1973. This was the first Concorde to have the same dimensions and shape as the production-series aircraft, with the extended tail cone and thrust reverser buckets. Preserved and displayed at Museé Delta, Orly Airport, Paris.

Total number of flights: 314 (189 supersonic)

**Hours flown: 656 hrs 37 min
(280 hrs 49 min supersonic)**

CONCORDE 201 F-WTSB – THIS aircraft was designated, along with 202, as a 'production test' aircraft; neither entered into airline service. 'SB first flew on December 6 1973 at Toulouse, where she is now on display outside the Airbus (formerly, Aerospatiale) headquarters.
**Total number of flights: 423
(247 supersonic)
Hours flown: 909 hrs 52 min
(339 hrs 25 min supersonic)**

CONCORDE 202 G-BBDG – FIRST flown on February 13 1974, this was the fastest Concorde and flew the greatest number of hours of any aircraft in the test and development fleet. Initially stored in the open at Filton, it was eventually placed in a specially constructed hangar where it was used as a source of spares after its acquisition by British Airways in 1984. Not on public view, it remained in the hangar minus its engines, vertical fin and rudder assembly, and its nose and visor assembly that had been used to replace the damaged nose section on G-BOAF following a ground-handling accident at Heathrow.

After being offered to the museum close to where many of her parts were built, she was dismantled and transported by road from Filton to her new home in May and June 2004. After re-assembly, repainting and interior refurbishment, she was opened to the public in the summer of 2006 at the Brooklands Museum, Weybridge, Surrey.
**Total number of flights: 633
(374 supersonic)
Hours flown: 1282 hrs 09 min
(514 hrs 09 min supersonic)**

CONCORDE 203 F-BTSC – PREVIously registered F-WTSC. This aircraft made its maiden flight on January 31 1975 at Toulouse. It was destroyed along with the loss of all on board, and four persons on the ground, when it crashed shortly after taking of from Paris-Charles de Gaulle airport on July 25 2000.
**Hours flown: 11,989 hrs
Total landings: 3,978**

CONCORDE 204 G-BOAC – FIRST flown on February 27 1975, this was the heaviest in the British Airways Concorde fleet. Subsequent aircraft were lighter, as the design was refined

still further. G-BOAC was unofficially considered to be the flagship of the fleet as it bore the initials of the airline's predecessor, BOAC. Placed on public display at Manchester airport.

Hours flown: 22,260 hrs 11 min
Total landings: 7,730
Supersonic flights: 6,761

CONCORDE 205 F-BVFA – WAS ALSO registered N94FA for the Braniff International lease in 1979. Now on display at the Smithsonian National Air and Space Museum's Steven F Udvar-Hazy Center, Dulles airport,

Washington DC. This aircraft made its maiden flight from Toulouse on October 27 1975.

Hours flown: 17,824 hrs
Total landings: 6,780
Supersonic flights: 5,504

CONCORDE 206 G-BOAA – FIRST flown on November 5 1975, this was the first Concorde to be delivered to British Airways. During the Braniff International lease in 1979/80, it bore the dual British/USA registrations G-N94AA/N94AA.This aircraft was not given the post-Paris crash modifications.

ABOVE Concorde arrives at its final destination at The Museum of Flight in Edinburgh. The last decommissioned Concorde G-BOAA arrived at its new home heralded by pipers after its long trek across country on a road specially built by the British Army

Dismantled and transported on a barge, by river and sea, to East Fortune, Scotland, she was re-assembled and is on public display, under cover.

Hours flown: 22,768 hrs 56 min
Total landings: 8,064
Supersonic flights: 6,842

CONCORDE 207 F-BVFB – FIRST flew March 6 1976. Was registered N94FB during the lease by Braniff International in 1979/80. Spectacularly displayed, together with a Tu-144 'Konkordski' above the roof of the Auto & Technik Museum, Sinsheim, Germany, where both aircraft are open to the public. This is the only place where both types of supersonic airliner can be seen together.

Hours flown: 14,771 hrs
Total landings: 5,473
Supersonic flights: 4,791

CONCORDE 208 G-BOAB – MADE its maiden flight on May 18 1976. Was registered as G-N94AB during 1979/80 for the Braniff International lease. Not modified to the post-Paris accident standard and never flew after that event. Temporarily stored alongside Runway 23 at London Heathrow and not open to the public. This aircraft is scheduled to become the focal point of the new Terminal 5.

Hours flown: 22,296 hrs 55 min
Total landings: 7,810
Supersonic flights: 6,688

CONCORDE 209 F-BVFC – FIRST flew on July 9 1976. During the Braniff International lease in 1979/80 was registered as N94FC. This aircraft was marooned in New York for three months following the Paris accident. Made the final supersonic flight by Air France when delivered, via the Bay of Biscay, to the Airbus factory at Toulouse, where she will eventually be displayed in a museum, together with Concorde 201 F-WTSB.

Hours flown: 14,332 hrs
Total landings: 4,358
Supersonic flights: 4,200

CONCORDE 210 G-BOAD – MAIDEN flight was made on August 25 1976. Was jointly registered as G-N94AD / N94AD for the 1979/80 Braniff International lease period. During 1979, one side of this aircraft was painted in the livery of Singapore Airlines, who operated a joint service with British Airways. G-BOAD also flew in formation with the Royal Air Force Red Arrows team for the flypast in honour of the Golden Jubilee of Her Majesty Queen Elizabeth II, on June 4 2002. This aircraft is on loan to the Intrepid Air and Space Museum, New York where it was on display to the public, parked on a pontoon moored to a pier alongside the Intrepid aircraft carrier. During renovation of the museum, G-BOAD was transferred to the Aviator Sports and Recreation facility at Floyd Bennett Field, New York, on December 22 2006 where it will remain for around 18 months to two years, on public display. It is not known at present when this aircraft will return to the Intrepid Museum.

Hours flown: 23,397 hrs 25 min
Total landings: 8,406
Supersonic flights: 7,010

CONCORDE 211 F-BVFD – FIRST flew on February 10 1977. Leased to Braniff International in 1979/80 when it was registered as N94FD. This aircraft underwent major repairs after a heavy landing at Dakar, in November 1977, in which its tail bumper wheel assembly was crushed. Withdrawn from service when surplus to requirements after the Paris-Dakar-Rio de Janeiro route ceased. Subsequently broken up, in 1994, at Paris-Charles de Gaulle airport

because of serious corrosion after standing outside for 12 years. The following year, an anonymous American purchased its nose assembly for around £32,000. The remains of the fuselage lie open, and unprotected, near Dugny, at Le Bourget airport, Paris.

Hours flown: 5,814 hrs
Total landings: 1,929
Supersonic flights: 1,807

CONCORDE 212 G-BOAE – FIRST flight was on March 17 1977. Became G-N94AE when leased to Braniff International in 1979/80. Retired to Grantley Adams airport, Barbados, West Indies, where it arrived on November 17 2003. Initially housed in a temporary shelter, it is hoped that it will later be displayed in a permanent visitor facility.

Hours flown: 23,376 hrs 7 min
Total landings: 8,383
Supersonic flights: 7,003

CONCORDE 213 F-BTSD – WAS first registered F-WJAM when it flew on its maiden flight on June 26 1978. Registered as F-BTSD when leased by its manufacturer Aerospatiale to Air France in September 1978, who later purchased the aircraft outright on October 23 1980. It was also involved in the Braniff International lease arrangement in 1979/80 when it bore the registration N94SD. F-BTSD holds the world records for the fastest round the-world flights in both directions; eastbound (32 hrs 49 min 03 sec, set on October 12/13 1992) and westbound (31 hrs 27 min 49 sec, set on August 15/16 1005). Was temporarily painted in a special blue Pepsi-Cola livery in April 1995 for product re-branding publicity. On display at the French Air and Space Museum, Le Bourget, Paris, alongside the prototype Concorde 001.

Hours flown: 12,974 hrs
Total landings: 5,135
Supersonic flights: 3,672

CONCORDE 214 G-BOAG – FIRST flew as a non-customer 'white tail', registered as G-BFKW to its owner, British Aerospace, on April 21 1979. Later leased by British Airways, it was grounded for a year following hydraulic system contamination that caused engine intake ramp failure, leading to engine surges. After a £1 million repair bill, it re-entered service as G-BOAG in

February 1981. Now retired to the Museum of Flight at Seattle, Washington, it made its final flight on November 5 2003.

Hours flown: 16,239 hrs 27 min
Total landings: 5,633
Supersonic flights: 5,066

CONCORDE 215 F-BVFF – MADE its maiden flight on December 26 1978, registered as F-WJAN to its manufacture, Aerospatiale. Re-registered as F-BVFF when delivered to Air France on October 23 1980. This aircraft was part way through its major 'D' check when the withdrawal from service was announced. F-BVFF was cosmetically re-assembled after work on the check had been stopped. Now located at Paris-Charles de Gaulle airport, where it

is displayed in a take-off pose on a plinth near the airport entrance road.

Hours flown: 12,421 hrs
Total landings: 4,259
Supersonic flights: 3,734

CONCORDE 216 G-BOAF – FIRST flew on April 20 1979, registered as G-BFKX to British Aerospace. Was re-registered as G-N94AF for its part in

the Braniff International lease programme. Became G-BOAF in June 1980, when registered to British Airways. Was the first aircraft to carry the British Airways 'Utopia' scheme known officially as Chatham Historic Dockyard, but generally referred to as the 'Union Flag' scheme. The first in the Concorde fleet to sustain a rudder failure, it was also the lead aircraft in the fleet to be fitted with the kevlar fuel tank liners and other modifications after the Paris accident. The last Concorde to be built, it was also the last to fly when, on November 26 2003, it landed into retirement at Filton, for display as part of the Bristol Aero Collection. Plans are in place for it to be displayed in a purpose-built exhibition hall on the north side of Filton airfield.

Hours flown: 18,257 hrs
Total landings: 6,045
Supersonic flights: 5,639

Postscript to Retirement

IN PARIS, A SMALL BUT DEDI-cated group of French volunteers have applied their engineering skills in an attempt to maintain Concorde 213 F-BTSD in near airworthy condition. Against all odds, and with no realistic chance of success, they carry out regular tests on her hydraulic and electrical systems in the hope that, one day, Concorde will once again take to the skies. All those who have an emotional attachment to this beautiful aircraft wish them well in their endeavours.

LEFT F-BVFA taxis at Dulles International Airport after which it will be on permanent display in the Smithsonian Institution's National Air and Space Museum

Chapter 11

Concorde Milestones

1956 – *November 5:* Britain established a Supersonic Transport Aircraft Committee (STAC) to study the feasibility of building a supersonic transport (SST) airliner.

1959 – *March 9:* Studies for two supersonic airliners to cruise at Mach 1.2 and Mach 2.0 recommended by STAC.

1961 – First discussions held between British Aircraft Corporation (BAC) and Sud-Aviation at Weybridge and Paris during June and July.

1962 – President Charles de Gaulle of France called for Britain and France to co-operate in building a supersonic airliner. Specification for joint venture Mach 2.0 airliner released in October.

November 29 – Draft treaty signed by Britain and France.

1963 – *January 13:* First use of 'Concorde', in relation to the project, by President de Gaulle. *June 3:* Options to purchase six aircraft signed by Pan American Airlines. *October 24:* Model of the proposed Anglo-French Concord (without an 'e') shown to the press at Filton, Bristol.

1964 – *March:* First contracts placed with main contractors BAC and Aerospatiale for the airframe, and Rolls-Royce and SNECMA for the engines. *May 1:* Maiden flight of the BAC 221 ogee-delta wing experimental aircraft at Filton. *November 19:* Britain's new Labour government announced

Britain's withdrawal from the project.

1965 – *January 20:* Labour government reverses its decision for Britain to withdraw from the SST project. *April:* First metal cut for first two prototype aircraft. *May:* Pre-production aircraft design frozen. *September 11:* Airframe construction commenced at Filton.

1966 – *March:* First static test centre-wing and fuselage assembly delivered to CEAT at Toulouse. *April:* Commencement of final assembly of French prototype 001 at Toulouse. First test run of Olympus 593 complete with

HIS EXCELLENCY
GEOFFROY de COURCEL

R. HON JULI

ABOVE A pilot in a flight simulator

reheat and exhaust assembly by SNECMA at Melun-Villaroche, France. Concorde flight simulator commissioned at Toulouse. *August:* Commencement of final assembly of British prototype 002 at Filton.

September 9: First flight test of Vulcan/Olympus 593 aircraft at Filton. *December:* Fatigue test fuselage assembly delivered to RAE Farnborough.

1967 – Design changes incorporated into pre-production aircraft 01 and 02;

new nose & visor and longer rear fuselage. *February:* Full-scale interior mock-up shown to prospective purchaser airlines at Filton. *April:* First test run of Olympus 593 engine and exhaust assembly in high-altitude chamber at Saclay, France. *May:* Concorde purchase options totalled 74 from 16 airlines. *December 11:* Rollout of first prototype 001 at Toulouse.

1968 – *January:* Vulcan/Olympus test aircraft reached 100 flying hours. *February:* British government loan of £125 million granted to cover production launch costs. *August:* Concorde 001 first taxy trials at Toulouse. *September 19:* Rollout of Concorde 002 at Filton. *December:* Olympus 593 logged 5,000 hours ground test time. *December 31:* Tu-144 'Konkordski' made first flight at Zhukovski, USSR.

1969 – *March:* Official approval given to build nine aircraft; two prototypes, two pre-production aircraft, two static test airframes (all retrospectively) and three production aircraft. *March 2:* Maiden flight of Concorde 001 at Toulouse. *April 9:* Maiden flight of Concorde 002 at Filton. *June:* Together, 001 and 002 make their first public appearance at Paris Air Show. *October:* Concorde 001 exceeded Mach 1.0 for the first time. *November 8:* Pilots from Air France, BOAC, Pan-Am & TWA each took the controls of 001. *November 12:* First night landing.

1970 – *February:* Olympus 593 ran continuously for 300 hours on ground test bed, equivalent to almost 100 transatlantic crossings. *March 25:* 002 flew at Mach 1.0 for the first time. *May:* New thrust-reverser engine nozzle specified for production models. *September 1:* 002 appeared at Farnborough Air Show. *September 13:* 002 landed at London Heathrow where local residents complained about noise. *November 4:* 001 achieved Mach 2.0. *November 12:* 002 reached Mach 2.0.

1971 – *January:* Total of 100 flights completed jointly by 001 and 002. April: Authority given for additional four production aircraft. *May:* First Concorde automatic landing made by 001. *June:* Total Concorde flight time reached 500 hours. Olympus 593 in-flight and test bed combined running time reached 10,000 hours. *August:* Concorde flight time at Mach 2.0 reached 100 hours. *September 20:* First pre-production Concorde 01 G-AXDN rolled out at Filton. *December 14:* US Federal

Aviation Agency (FAA) stated Concorde was within US airport noise limits. *December 17:* 01 made first flight. *December 21:* All three flyable Concorde aircraft were airborne, simultaneously.

1972 – *February:* Concorde 02 F-WTSA structurally completed. 01 G-AXDN flew at Mach 1.0 for the first time. *April 13:* Production of a further six aircraft approved. *May 18:* Concorde flight-testing reached a total of 1,000 flying hours. *June 2:* Far East demonstration tour commenced by 002. *July 24:* China signed preliminary option to buy two aircraft. *July 28:* BOAC ordered five aircraft and Air France ordered four. *August 28:* China added one more aircraft to its options. *September 28:* Concorde 02 rolled out at Toulouse. *October 5:* Iran Air placed purchase agreement for two aircraft plus an option for one more. *October 26:* United Air Lines cancelled its options for six aircraft. *December 11:* British government approved production loan increase to £350 million.

1973 – *January 10:* 02 maiden flight at Toulouse. *January 31:* Pan-Am & TWA cancelled all their options to purchase Concorde. *March 29:* Continental Airlines also cancelled all their options.

June 3: Tu-144 crashed at Paris Air Show. *September 18:* 02 left Paris for the opening of Dallas-Fort Worth airport, Texas. On its return, on Sep 25, it broke the record between Washington and Paris with a flying time of 3 hrs 33 min. *October 19:* Prototype 001 retired to French Air Museum, Le Bourget, Paris. *December 6:* Concorde 201 F-WTSB, first production series aircraft maiden flight from Toulouse.

1974 – *February 13:* Concorde 202 G-BBDG maiden flight from Filton. *July 19:* British and French governments limited production to 16 aircraft. *September 12:* Flight testing reached total of 3,000 hours. *October 20:* 02 left London on six-day tour of US West Coast & South America. *October 21:* Total of 1,000 hours of supersonic flight achieved.

1975 – *January 31:* Concorde 203 F-WTSC maiden flight. *February 27:* Concorde 204 G-BOAC maiden flight. *April 25:* Air France commenced a two-week flight crew-training programme at Dakar. *May 6:* Brazil agreed to let Air France Concorde aircraft carry out scheduled flights to its territory. *May 28:* Special category CofA awarded to Concorde 203 for it to commence route-proving flights. Registration changed from F-WTSC to F-BTSC. *June 19:* British Airways commenced flight crew training at RAF Fairford. *June 30:* Concorde 204 received its special category CofA. *September 1:* Concorde 204

G-BOAC became first aircraft to make four transatlantic crossings in one day between London and Gander. *October 9:* Full French CofA awarded to Concorde. *October 14:* Reservations taken for start of scheduled services on Jan 26 1976 to

Bahrain (British Airways) and Rio de Janeiro (Air France). *October 25:* Concorde 205 F-BVFA made her maiden flight in the new Air France livery. *November 5:* Concorde 206 G-BOAA maiden flight. Concorde received its full British CofA. *December* *18:* United States implemented a six-month ban on Concorde landing in the USA. *December 19:* Air France took delivery of its first supersonic airliner, Concorde 205 F-BVFA.

1976 – *January 6:* Air France took delivery of its second Concorde 203

F-BTSC. *January 21:* British Airways took delivery of Concorde 206 G-BOAA, its first supersonic airliner. *January 21:* Concorde entered airline service, on routes to Bahrain and Rio de Janeiro. *February 4:* The US authorised British Airways and Air France to each operate two Concorde services per day to New York, and one service each, per day, to Washington for trial period of 16 months. *February 13:* British Airways took delivery of its second Concorde 204 G-BOAC. *March 4:* Concorde 002 G-BSST retired to Fleet Air Arm Museum, Yeovilton. *March 6:* Concorde 207 F-BVFB maiden flight. *March 11.* New York and New Jersey port authority banned Concorde. *April 8:* Air France took delivery of third Concorde 207 F-BVFB. *April 9:* Air France commenced weekly service to Caracas, Venezuela, via the Azores. *May 18:* Concorde 208 G-BOAB on her maiden flight from Filton, reached Mach 2.05 at 63,000 feet. *May 20:* Concorde 02 F-WTSA retired to Orly airport, Paris. *May 24:* Two Concordes, one each from Air France and British Airways, made simultaneous landings on parallel runways at Washington-Dulles. *July 9:* Concorde 209 F-BVFC maiden flight. *August 13:* Air France took delivery of its fourth Concorde 209 F-BVFC. *August 25:* Concorde 210 G-BOAD maiden flight. *September 30:* British Airways took delivery of its third aircraft, Concorde 208 G-BOAB. *November 30:* Closure of Fairford flight test centre. *December 6:*

British Airways took delivery of its fourth aircraft, Concorde 210 G-BOAD. *December 8:* Air France returned Concorde 203 F-BTSC to Aerospatiale.

1977 – *January 21:* Anniversary of first year in airline service, having carried 45,000 passengers over almost 3.5 million miles. *February 10:* Concorde 211 maiden flight. Braniff International applied to US Civil Aeronautics Board to operate a six days per week subsonic Concorde service between Washington and Dallas-Fort Worth. *March 17:* Concord 212 G-BOAE maiden flight. *March 26:* Air France took delivery of its fifth Concorde, 211 F-BVFD. *May 21:* On 50th anniversary of Lindbergh's Spirit of St Louis flight from New York to Paris in 33 hrs 29 min, a Concorde flew the route in 3 hrs 44 min. *July 20:* British Airways took delivery of its fifth Concorde, 212 G-BOAE. *August 20:* Concorde 01 G-AXDN retired to Duxford. *October 19:* First Concorde landing in New York made by Air France with Concorde 201 F-WTSB. *November 22:* Air France and British Airways commenced services to New York from Paris and London, respectively. *December 9:* Joint British Airways/Singapore Airlines services to Singapore, via Bahrain, began. *December 13:* Malaysia bans Concorde from its airspace.

1978 – *January 21:* Concorde celebrates second year in service with a total of 129.000 passengers carried. *April 21:* Concorde 214 G-BFKW maiden flight. *June 26:* Concorde 213 F-WJAM maiden flight. *August 10:* British

RIGHT British Airways' Concorde arrives at John F Kennedy Airport

RIGHT British Airways' Concorde arrives at John F Kennedy Airport

Airways carried their 100,000th Concorde passenger. *September 1:* Concorde cleared for Category III automatic landings. *September 18:* Air France took delivery of their sixth Concorde, 213 F-WJAM, re-registered as F-BTSD. *September 20:* Air France began a twice-weekly Paris-Mexico City, via Washington DC. *November 21:* Concorde's first anniversary of services to New York. *December 26:* Concorde 215 F-WJAN maiden flight.

1979 – *January:* Five Air France Concordes given US registrations, and five British Airways aircraft registered with dual British/US numbers, ready for leased Braniff subsonic services. *January 9:* Concorde awarded US type CofA. *January 12:* Braniff International commenced subsonic Washington-Dulles to Dallas-Fort Worth services. *January 21:* Concorde on its third anniversary in service had completed 21,700 flying hours and carried almost 300,000 passengers. *January 24:* Resumption of joint service to Singapore. *April 20:* Last production Concorde 216 G-BFKX maiden flight. *September 21:* British and French governments announced that no more Concorde aircraft would be built. *December 14:* Concorde 216 re-registered with dual US/British identities G-N94AF/G-BOAF. *December 16:* British Airways Concorde flew a London-New York sector in 2 hrs 59 min.

1980 – *February 6:* British Airways took delivery of its sixth Concorde, 214 G BFKW. *June 1:* Braniff subsonic services discontinued. *June 13:* British Airways took delivery of its seventh, and last, Concorde G-BOAF the day after its US registration was cancelled. *October 23:* Air France took delivery of its seventh, and last, Concorde 215

F-WJAN, now registered F-BVFF. *November 1:* Joint British Airways/Singapore Airlines services to Singapore discontinued.

1981 – *January 21:* Concorde completed five years in service, totalling 50,000 flying hours over 15,800 flights and had carried 700,000 passengers. *February 9:* Concorde 214 G-BKFW re-registered as G-BOAG. *April 14:* House of Commons committee reported their dissatisfaction with project costs. *July:* British government described the committee's criticisms as "…unwarranted". *September 11:* Anglo-French summit meeting held to consider the future of Concorde. *October 29:* British and French ministers met in London to consider (a) cancellation of the project, (b) a phased run down, (c) indefinite continuation of the project.

1982 – *March 31:* Air France discontinued services to Caracas and Rio de Janeiro. *May 1:* British Airways established a Concorde Division responsible for the profitability of Concorde operations. *May 6:* Ministerial meeting held in Paris to discuss cost reduction of Concorde project. *August:* British government informed British Airways of the decision to cease funding of Concorde airframe and engine manufacturers in Britain. *October:* Sir John King, chairman of British Airways, replied that the airline would look at funding Concorde support costs from revenue. *October 29:* Air France ceased Concorde services to Washington. *November:* British Airways set up a group to review Concorde support costs.

1983 – *January 1:* Fastest-ever Concorde flight from New York to London in 2 hrs 56 min.

1984 – *March 27:* New Concorde service commenced to Miami, via Washington-Dulles. *March 31:* British government effectively withdrew from Concorde project with British Airways assuming responsibility for British manufacturers' support costs. *September 11:* Concorde 208 G-BOAB set distance record for the type of 3,965 nautical miles between Washington DC and Nice, France.

1985 – *February 13:* New London–Sydney record time of 17 hrs 3 min established by Concorde on a charter flight. *March 28:* New London–Cape Town record of 8 hrs 8 min set on a commercial charter. *April 25:* New British Airways livery and interior unveiled on Concorde 214 G-BOAG. *December 19:* Highest-ever ground speed in commercial service of 1,488 miles per hour set by Concorde 204 G-BOAC.

1986 – *January 21:* Tenth anniversary in service. Reached a total of 71,000 supersonic, passenger-carrying flying hours. *April 5:* First Concorde charter flight to New Zealand. *November 8-23:* First round-the-world charter flight in total flight time of 31 hrs 51 min.

1987 – *September 6:* New transatlantic record of 1 hr 35 min set between Newfoundland and the west coast of Ireland. *October 5:* British Airways carried their one-millionth passenger, Patrick Mannix of Reuters, on transatlantic scheduled services. *November 22:* Concorde celebrated 10 years of operations into JFK-New York by carrying the world land speed record holder, Richard Noble, across the Atlantic a record three times in one day. *December 12:* British Airways commenced a weekly Concorde service to Barbados for the winter season.

1988 – Concorde 206 G-BOAA became the first of its type to undergo a 12,000 flying hours check. *May:* Concorde 202 G-BBDG placed in

purpose-built hangar at Filton for use as a spare parts Christmas tree.

1989 – *March 2:* Aerospatiale hosted party to celebrate the 20th anniversary of Concorde 001's maiden flight. *April 12:* Concorde 216 G-BOAF lost a section of rudder between New Zealand and Sydney.

1990 – *May 5:* Plans announced by Aerospatiale and British Aerospace for a Concorde successor. *August 1:* Air France Concorde 205 F-BVFA completed its major check after 11,650 flying hours and 12 million miles

covered. *September 7:* Scale model of Concorde installed at main entrance to Heathrow airport.

1991 – *January:* A second British Airways Concorde rudder failed in flight. *January 21:* Concorde in service for 15 years.

1992 – *March 21:* Third Concorde rudder failed as a British Airways flight neared New York. *May 15:* British Airways announced that all seven of its Concordes would have their rudders replaced.

1993 – *March 26:* Barbara Harmer, a British Airways First Officer, became the first female Concorde pilot. *May 21:* G-BOAF became the first British Airways Concorde to be refurbished and re-liveried in a £1 million per aircraft programme. *November 19:* Concorde 206 G-BOAA was fitted with the first of the new rudders that had reportedly cost £1 million to re-design and manufacture.

1994 – *March 2:* 25th anniversary of Concorde 001 F-WTSS maiden flight at Toulouse. *August:* Cracks found in the rear spar web of a Concorde wing were repaired. Three cabin outer windows failed at Mach 2.0 and 57,000 feet.

1995 – *May 29:* British Concorde designer, Sir Archibald Russell CBE FRS, died, aged 90. *September:* Olympus 593 engine achieved 500,000 hours flight time. *October:* Announcement that British and French airworthiness authorities are to decide in the following year whether any modifications are necessary to extend life of Concorde to 8,500 Reference Flights.

1996 – *January:* TCAS avoidance system fitted to comply with US regulations. *January 21:* Concorde celebrated 20 years in airline service. *February:* Decision made that no modifications were necessary for Concorde Life Extension Programme. Six maintenance schedule changes were the only additional requirements. *April 2:* Air France Concorde 213 F-BTSD was

painted in bright blue Pepsi-Cola livery and displayed at London Gatwick airport to launch the new drinks can design.

1997 – British Airways began repainting its Concorde fleet in the new corporate livery known as the 'Historic Chatham Dockyard' scheme.

1998 – *May 24:* G-BOAC had a failure of its No.3 left elevon control surface, similar to the previous rudder failures. *October 8:* G-BOAC had a failure of its newer-design lower rudder, en route to New York.

1999 – *May:* British Airways unveiled their new Concorde fleet interior that was designed by Terence Conran.

2000 – *July 23:* British Airways temporarily grounded Concorde 212

G-BOAE after cracks were found in non-critical areas of its wing structure. *July 25:* Air France Concorde 203 F-BTSC crashed shortly after take-off from Paris, with the loss of all on board and four persons on the ground. *July 26:* British Airways resumed Concorde flights following the previous day's accident. *August 15:* British Airways Concorde ordered to return to its stand by the airline while taxiing for take-off. Decision taken after learning that the withdrawal of the CofA was imminent. *August 16:* UK CAA and the French DGAC both formally withdraw CofA for Concorde. *August 31:* Preliminary report found that a tyre burst was the prime contributory cause of the accident. *September 7:* Anglo-French working group set up to explore possible ways to return Concorde to service. *September 21:* Air France flew the stranded Concorde 209 F-BVFC home from New York. *December 12:* The second crash investigation report to be published confirmed that burst tyre debris had caused a fuel tank to rupture.

2001 – *January:* British Airways begin modifications to Concorde 216 G-BOAF in preparation for possible return to service. Kevlar liners were

fitted to some of its fuel tanks. *March:* Brian Trubshaw OBE, CBE, former Chief Test Pilot of BAC, died aged 77. *April 11:* Air France Concorde 213 F-BTSD flew on air test following completion of D check. *June 7:* Announcement that new Michelin NZG (Near Zero Growth) main gear tyres will be fitted to all Concordes on return to service. *June 19:* Modifications completed on G-BOAF. *June 20:* Modifications to G-BOAE began at Heathrow. *July 17:* First supersonic verification flight completed by British Airways when G-BOAF landed at RAF Brize Norton after flying for 3 hrs 20 min. *July 25:* Memorial services held in Paris and at crash site, Gonesse, on first anniversary of F-BTSC tragedy. *August 16:* Formal application submitted to British and French authorities for re-certification of all modified Concorde aircraft. *August 24:* First Air France supersonic verification flight completed successfully by Concorde 207 F-BVFB. *August 27:* Second supersonic verification flight flown by F-BVFB at speeds up to Mach 2.0. *September 5:* British and French authorities return the CofA for all Concorde aircraft that have undergone the modification programme. *September 11:* The first passengers carried since the return of its CofA were flown by Concorde 216 G-BOAF on an Operational Assessment Flight. *September 28:* Concorde 212 G-BOAE completed its verification flight after modification. *October 5:* G-BOAF completed a second Operational Assessment Flight around the Bay of Biscay. *October 15:* Air France Concorde 207 F-BVFB completed its verification flight after modification. *October 16:* British Airways placed Concorde tickets on sale prior to return to service. *October 19:* Concorde 214 G-BOAG became the third British Airways aircraft to fly after modifications. *October 22:* Final Operational Assessment Flight made by Concorde 216 G-BOAF to New York before re-commencement of British Airways service. *October 29:* Air France made a return Operational Assessment Flight to New York with F-BVFB. This day, Prime Minister Tony Blair flew on Concorde to Washington DC to meet President George Bush. *December 19:* British Airways offered Concorde tickets to New York for £2002 to celebrate the New Year 2002. All sold in 3 minutes.

2002 – *January 12:* Final report published into the accident involving F-BTSC at Gonesse. This concluded that the tyre burst after running over debris on the runway. The damaged tyre shreds caused consequential damage to a fuel tank initiating a major leak. The subsequent, almost instantaneous, fire and loss of engine power resulted in the fatal crash. *January 29:* Concorde 210 G-BOAD completed its test flight after modification. *February 10:* G-BOAD resumed scheduled services to New York. *April 1:* British Airways now had four aircraft modified. *May:* Air France's final aircraft to undergo its major 12,000 hours check, F-BVFF, entered maintenance. *July 11:* British Airways fifth aircraft to be modified, Concorde 204 G-BOAC, rejoined the fleet after being grounded for 23 months. *August 25:* The 25th anniversary of the arrival of Concorde 01 G-AXDN was celebrated at Duxford. *November 22:* The 25th anniversary of Concorde services to New York. *November 27:* Concorde 212 G-BOAE rudder failed, the fifth on British Airways' fleet.

2003 – *February 25:* Air France had their first rudder failure, on Concorde 205 F-BVFA. This occurred at a similar total hours flown as that for British Airways first rudder failure in the 1980s. *March 2:* Death of Sir George Edwards, aged 94, former chairman of BAC, and a persuasive Concorde advocate. *April 10:* Simultaneous announcement by British Airways and Air France that Concorde would make its final passenger flight in October 2003. Air France later brought forward their cessation date to May 31. *April 11:* Richard Branson, Virgin Airlines' founder and chairman, announced he was prepared to buy the British Airways fleet for £1 per aircraft. He had claimed that his airline could run Concorde at a profit due to Virgin's greater efficiency. *May 31:* Final flights of Air France Concorde aircraft; F-BTSD flew the final New York-Paris service, and F-BVFB flew a charter flight around the Bay of Biscay. June 12: Concorde 205 F-BVFA flew into retirement at the Smithsonian Institute's new Air and Space Museum, at Washington-Dulles airport. *June 14:* Concorde 213 F-BTSD was retired to the Air and Space Museum, Le Bourget, Paris. *June 24:* Concorde 207 F-BVFB made its last flight to Karlsruhe-Baden Baden Airpark in south-west Germany. After partial disassembly, it was taken by road and canal barge, to the Auto & Technik Museum at Sinsheim. There, it was re-assembled, and hoisted into position

above the roof of the museum building. It can now be seen together with its Russian contemporary, the Tu-144. *June 27:* Concorde 209 F-BVFC operated the final Air France Concorde flight when it flew into retirement, at Toulouse. *July 26:* British Airways commenced their final Barbados summer schedules with G-BOAD. *August 30:* G-BOAC flew the last Barbados to London supersonic service. *October 1–14:* Farewell tour of North America flown by G-BOAG. *October 15:* Final scheduled New York to London service flown by G-BOAG. *October 20:* First UK farewell flight took place when G-BOAC visited Birmingham. *October 21:* G-BOAC farewell visit to Belfast. *October 22:* G-BOAG flew the farewell flight to Manchester. *October 23:* Farewell to Cardiff flown by G-BOAC. *October 24:* Final day in commercial service. G-BOAE flew a return Edinburgh farewell flight, G-BOAF flew the final Bay of Biscay round-trip charter, and G-BOAG flew the last scheduled supersonic service from New York. All three Concorde aircraft landed, in sequence, at Heathrow shortly after 4pm. *October 30:* British Airways announced the

retirement at the Museum of Flight, Seattle. *November 10:* Concorde 210 G-BOAD flew to New York's JFK airport, from where she was taken by barge to the Intrepid Sea, Air, and Space Museum, on the Hudson River. *November 17:* Concorde 212 G-BOAE flew into retirement at Grantley Adams airport, Barbados. *November 26:* Concorde 216 G-BOAF made the last-ever flight by this iconic aircraft. Flying supersonic for the last time over the Bay of Biscay, she made her final touchdown shortly after 1pm at the place where she, and all of the British-built Concorde aircraft were made, Filton, Bristol.

Epilogue

"Concorde will never really stop flying because it will live on in people's imagination." – *Jean-Cyril Spinetta, chairman of Air France.*

"Concorde was born from dreams, built with vision and operated with pride." – *Captain Mike Bannister, Chief Concorde Pilot, British Airways.*

LEFT To celebrate the Queen's Golden Jubilee, Concorde is joined by the Red Arrows

retirement homes for its Concorde fleet. *October 31:* Concorde 204 G-BOAC flew subsonically into retirement at Manchester airport. *November 3:* Concorde 214 G-BOAG flew to New York, en route to Seattle. *November 5:* G-BOAG flew supersonically over northern Canada en route to

The Little Book of Concorde

Credits and References

Internet:

http://www.aeroflight.co.uk

www.bakerlite.co.uk/concorde_comes_home.htm

www.britishairways.com

www.century-of-flight.net

http://christopherfrancis.co.uk/Concord.htm

www.concordesst.com

www.airliners.net

Books:

Concorde – Kev Darling, The Crowood Press

Concorde – The Complete Inside Story – Brian Trubshaw, Sutton Publishing

Flying Concorde – Brian Calvert, Airlife Publications